FISHING ALASKAN WATERS

by MARILYN CARTER

Published by Aladdin Publishing, July, 1981
Second Edition, June, 1983
Third Edition, May, 1986

Aladdin Publishing,
Box 364, Palmer, Alaska 99645

Printed in U.S.A.

ACKNOWLEDGEMENTS:
Alaska State Department of Fish and Game
United States Forest Service
and the Bureau of Land Management
For sources of information used to compile this book.

Art work, layout and design by Marilyn Carter
Aladdin Publishing

INTRODUCTION

The information in this fishing handbook has been gathered from a variety of sources. Most of the maps and a large percentage of the material contained in the schedules of salmon runs was taken from data compiled by the Alaska State Department of Fish and Game, and used with their kind permission.

This guide book has been written to furnish anglers with a permanent reference to all the freshwater sports fish in Alaskan waters.

Most important are the time schedules of the spawning runs of the five Pacific salmon (the king, silver, red, pink and chum) into the rivers and streams of this northern country.

The author has included the major fishing regions throughout the state, with information that should be helpful in finding the specific game fish wanted in any specific waterway.

The salmon run schedules are as accurate as possible to predict, considering the many variables present. Information on methods to use, what bait, lure, etc. are offered to the fisherman as a general rule only. Each lake, stream or coastal strip of beach has its own pecularities as to what the fish will strike, or at what depth fish can be found, etc.

Fishing Alaskan Waters by no means guarantees that an angler will limit out each time he or she enters the field. It should, however, be a great help in choosing the lake or stream to fish, and the methods to use to entice the wary critters to hit your lure.

The section of the book containing calendars for the salmon migratory runs and sports fish schedule will have listed only the *hot spots* for that particular fish. More detailed locations will be found in the *times of abundance* chart.

Keep in mind that emergency closure or change can happen at any time. This is particularly true for king salmon fishing. Whenever in doubt, check with the local office of the Department of Fish and Game.

Remember: The time schedules for these migratory salmon runs will vary, according to cyclic conditions, weather, and the salmon's built-in mechanism that triggers the start of the spawning run. This is nature's control and cannot be computerized by fishermen or the Alaska Department of Fish and Game.

GOOD LUCK AND GOOD FISHING!

FRONT COVER PHOTO
Fishing for Kings at Clear Creek, on the Talkeetna River.

BACK COVER PHOTO
Mount McKinley, looking over the Talkeetna River.

NOTICE

This handbook is meant to furnish the angler with a permanent reference as to areas for tne best fishing, maps showing specific waterway locations, the seasonal times of abundance, and methods to use.

ALWAYS CHECK THE STATE FISH AND GAME REGULATION BOOKLET FOR OPENING DATES, TACKLE RESTRICTIONS, STREAMS OPEN TO FISHING, ETC., FOR THE CURRENT SEASON.

Fishing dates in this handbook are for the times of abundance for that particular fish—unless otherwise noted.

ACCESSIBILITY TO FISHING AREAS

Many of Alaska's fishing areas can be reached by road. A highway map will show you the major waterways crossed by road systems. Be forewarned that you will be surrounded by many other fishermen, unless you are willing to hike a little further off the beaten path.

FLY - IN FISHING

Lake Hood in Anchorage offers many professional charter services, including Big Red's and Alaska Bush Carrier, (on the west lake shore.) You will beat the crowds, find a spot of peacefulness, and the fishing will be much better. Most of Alaska's cities and smaller towns will have charter service available.

RIVERBOAT SERVICES

Use this service from the numerous lodges throughout the state. Most of them will be located right on the rivers you want to fish. They also offer float and canoe trips in most localities. Boat rentals are sometimes available.

If you are new to Alaska, use the yellow pages of your telephone directory to find the service you need.

CONTENTS

HYPOTHERMIA.....6
ALASKA INDEX MAP.....9
FRESH WATER SECTION.....11
KING SALMON.....11
KING SALMON CALENDAR.....14
SILVER SALMON.....17
SILVER SALMON CALENDAR.....18
RED SALMON.....20
RED SALMON CALENDAR.....22
PINK SALMON.....24
PINK SALMON CALENDAR.....25
CHUM SALMON.....28
CHUM SALMON CALENDAR.....29
STEELHEAD.....30
STEELHEAD CALENDAR.....31
RAINBOW TROUT.....32
RAINBOW TROUT CALENDAR.....33
DOLLY VARDEN.....36
DOLLY VARDEN CALENDAR.....37
LAKE TROUT.....40
LAKE TROUT CALENDAR.....41
CUTTHROAT TROUT.....44
EASTERN BROOK TROUT.....45
ARCTIC CHAR.....46
ARCTIC CHAR CALENDAR.....47
ARCTIC GRAYLING.....48
ARCTIC GRAYLING CALENDAR.....49
NORTHERN PIKE.....52
NORTHERN PIKE CALENDAR.....53
SHEEFISH.....54
WHITEFISH.....55
BURBOT.....56
SALTWATER SECTION.....57
SALMON DERBIES STATEWIDE.....58
SALTWATER FISHING.....60
KING SALMON.....60
SEA-RUN TROUT.....62
HALIBUT.....63
ROCKFISH.....65
BOTTOMFISH.....65
EULACHON.....66
CLAMS.....67
CRAB.....68
MAP SECTION-STREAM FISHING.....71
ABBREVIATION TABLE-FISH SPECIES.....71
TABLE OF CONTENTS - MAP'S.....72 to 128
TIME OF ABUNDANCE CHART.....73

HYPOTHERMIA

Hypothermia is a rapid, progressive mental and physical collapse accompanying the chilling of the inner core of the human body. It is caused by exposure to cold, aggravated by wet, wind, and exhaustion. **IT IS THE NUMBER ONE KILLER OF OUTDOOR RECREATIONISTS.**

When your body begins to *lose heat* faster than it can produce it, two things happen. (1) You voluntarily exercise to stay warm. (2)Your body makes involuntary adjustments to preserve *normal temperatue* in the vital organs. Either of these responses drains your energy reserves. The only way to stop the drain is to reduce the degreee of exposure. If you are unable to do this, hypothermia occurs. RESULTS: Cold reaches the brain, depriving you of judgement and reasoning power. *You will not realize this is happening;* next, you will lose control of your hands. Without treatment, this internal temperature loss will lead to stupor, collapse, and finally death.

PRECAUTIONARY STEPS

1. ***Stay dry.*** Wet clothing loses 90% of its insulating value, wool loses less than other materials.
2. ***Beware the wind.*** It drives cold air under and through clothing, and multiplies the problems of staying dry.
3. ***Understand cold.*** Although the following is hard to believe, it is true that most hypothermia cases occur in air temperatures between 30 and 50 degrees. 50 degrees water is very cold; it does serious harm when held against the body by sopping wet clothing, this results in flushing body heat from the surface of the clothes.

If you cannot stay dry and warm under existing conditions, terminate the exposure. Turn back, get out of the wind and rain, build a fire. Concentrate on making your camp as comfortable and warm as possible.

NEVER IGNORE SHIVERING. This is warning that you are on the verge of hypothermia. **MAKE CAMP.**

Realize that when you stop exercising, your rate of body heat production instantly drops by 50% or more. Violent shivering may begin immediately. You may slip into hypothermia in a matter of minutes. **FORESTALL THIS** by making camp while you still have a reserve of energy remaining.

DETECT HYPOTHERMIA EARLY. Watch for the following symptoms in yourself and other members of your party:

1. Uncontollable fits of shivering.
2. Vague, slow, slurred speech.
3. Memory lapses, incoherence.
4. Frequent stumbling.
5. Immobile, fumbling hands.
6. Drowsiness.
7. Apparent exhaustion, inability to get up after a rest.

TREATMENT:

1. Get the victim out of the wind and rain.
2. Strip off all wet clothing.
3. Give patient warm drinks; get him into dry clothes and a warm sleeping bag. Well-wrapped, warm rocks or canteens will speed recovery.
4. If patient is semi-conscious or worse:
   a. Try to keep him awake.
   b. Leave him stripped, put him in a sleeping bag with another person (also stripped). If a double sleeping bag is available, put victim between two warm donors. **SKIN TO SKIN CONTACT** is the most effective treatment.
5. Build a fire to warm the camp.

NOTES ON EQUIPMENT:

Choose rainclothes that are proof against wind-driven rain and that cover head, neck body and legs. Polyurethane nylon is best. Ponchos are poor protection in wind.
Take woolen clothing for hypothermia weather: two piece woolen underwear or long wool pants, and sweater or shirt. Use a knit cap that can protect neck and chin.
A stormproof tent affords best shelter; include plastic sheeting and nylon twine for rigging additional foul-weather shelter.
Carry trail food: candy, nuts, jerky, etc. Keep nibbling during hypothermia weather.
Take a gas campstove or a plumber's candle, flammable paste, or other reliable firestarter.

ANGLER'S
HABITAT

LOCATED IN THE COUNTRY VILLAGE MALL

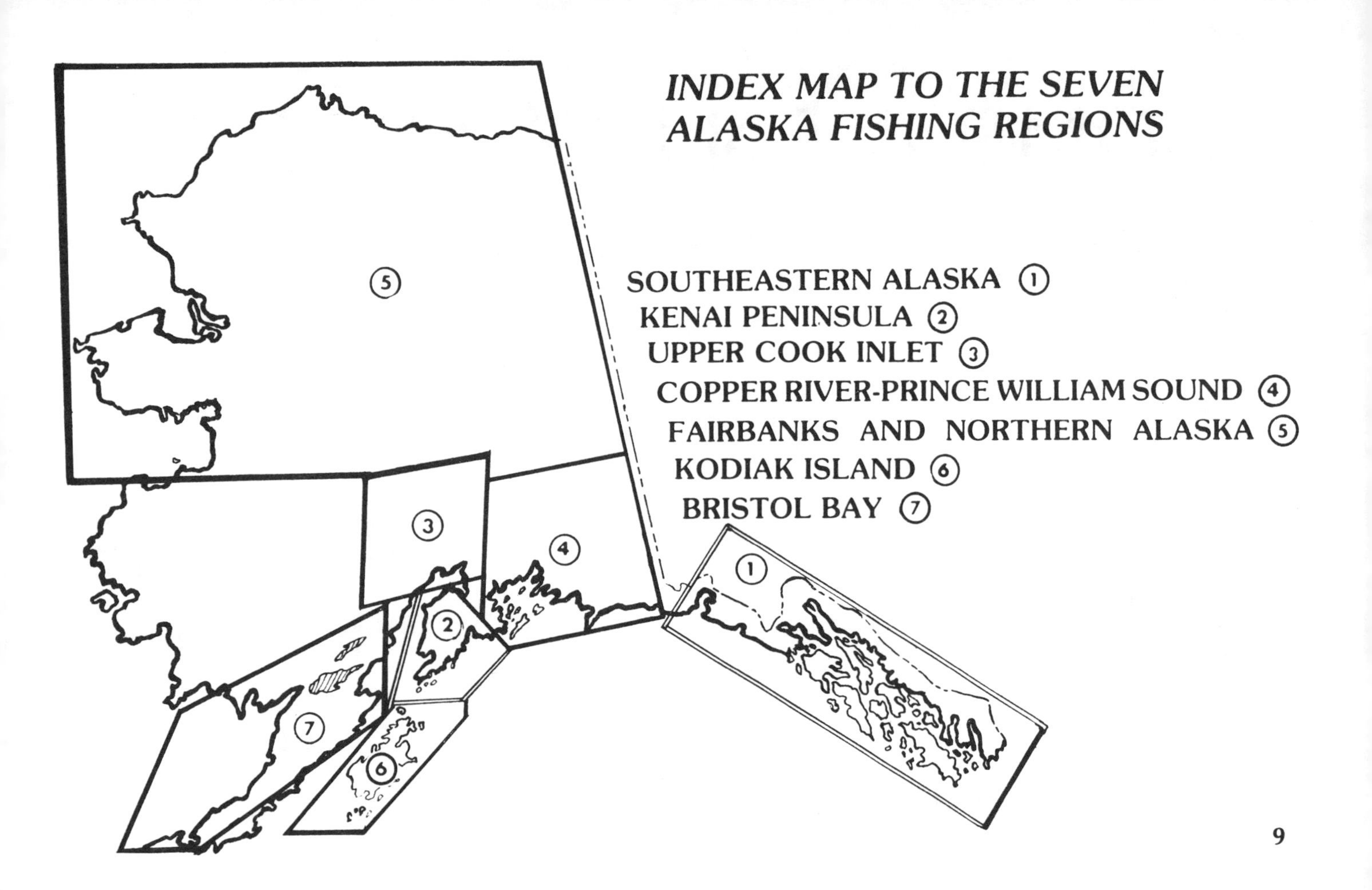
INDEX MAP TO THE SEVEN
ALASKA FISHING REGIONS
SOUTHEASTERN ALASKA 1
KENAI PENINSULA 2
UPPER COOK INLET 3
COPPER RIVER-PRINCE WILLIAM SOUND 4
FAIRBANKS AND NORTHERN ALASKA 5
KODIAK ISLAND 6
BRISTOL BAY 7
5
3
4
2
1
7
6

FRESH WATER SECTION

Calendar of Salmon Runs

King ● Silver ● Red ● Pink ● Chum

Calendar of Sports Fish

Steelhead
Rainbow
Dolly Varden
Lake Trout
Cutthroat Trout
Eastern Brook Trout

Arctic Char
Arctic Grayling
Whitefish
Northern Pike
Sheefish
Burbot

WHERE, WHEN AND HOW TO CATCH 'EM

KING SALMON

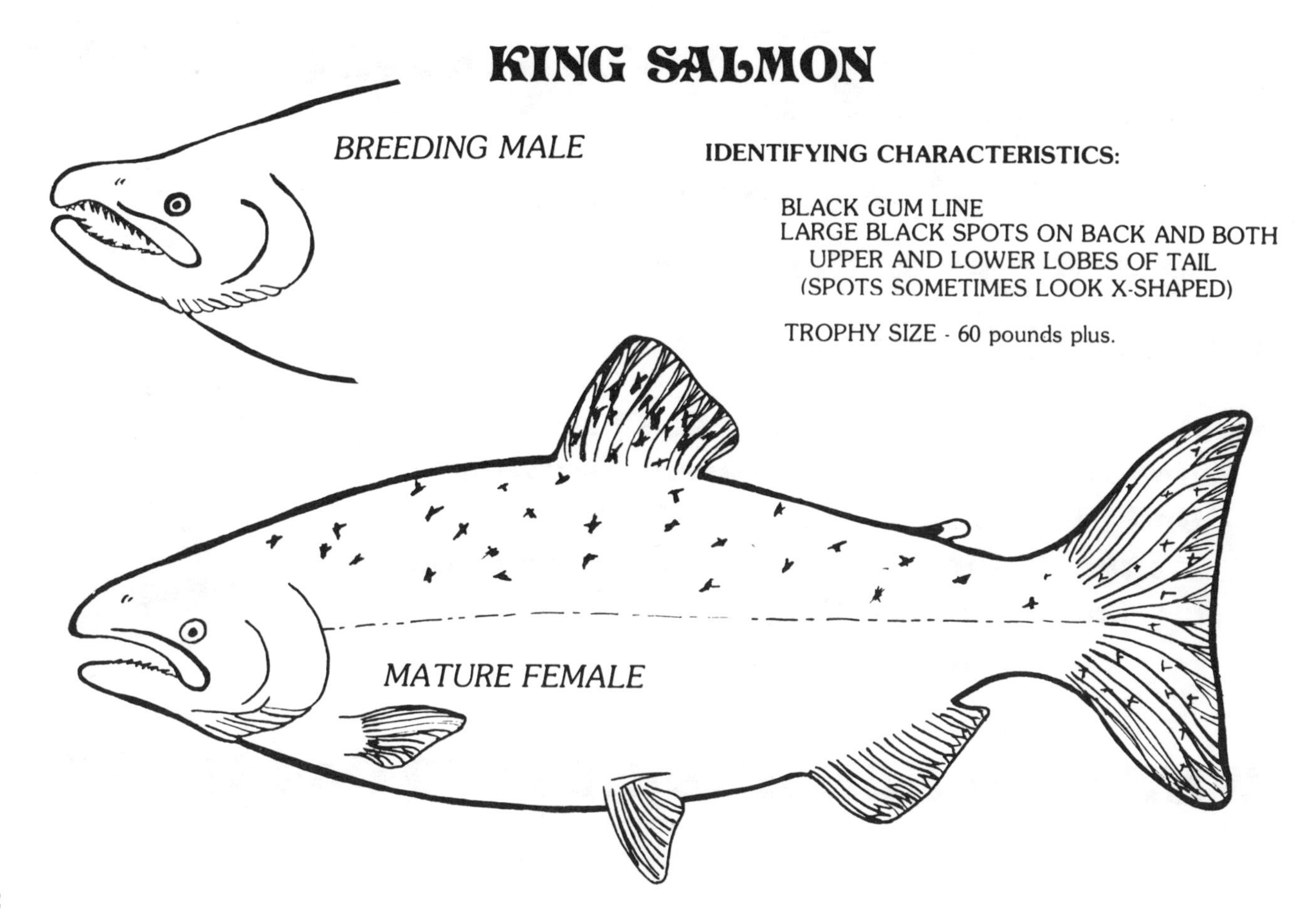

IDENTIFYING CHARACTERISTICS:

BLACK GUM LINE
LARGE BLACK SPOTS ON BACK AND BOTH UPPER AND LOWER LOBES OF TAIL (SPOTS SOMETIMES LOOK X-SHAPED)

TROPHY SIZE - 60 pounds plus.

KING SALMON

(Also called Chinook, Spring salmon, Quinnat, Tyee, Tule, and Blackmouth.)

RANGE AND DESCRIPTION

This behemoth of the salmon family ranges in Alaska from the Southeastern panhandle to the Yukon River. Major spawning runs occur on the Yukon, Kuskokwim, Nashagak, Susitna, Kenai, Copper, Alsek, Taku and Stikine Rivers; with important runs up the tributaries of these rivers, and many smaller streams in the state.

The King salmon is the longest-lived of the Pacific salmon, and the largest. Weights of over 30 pounds are common, with reports of an occasional fish of 100 pounds and more being caught. The sports tackle record is a 97 pounder caught at the mouth of the Kenai River in 1985 by Les Anderson of Soldotna, Alaska. A 126-pounder was taken in a fish trap near Petersburg in 1949 and to date is the established commercial record.

Feeder kings can occasionally be caught throughout the year along Alaska's coastline, although the spawning schools in most areas don't arrive at the mouths of their home streams until spring. The richest of the king salmon are those who make the more than 2,000 mile migration up the Yukon River to spawn in the extreme headwaters of the Yukon Territory. This spawning run takes 60 days, (beginning in June) and the extra stored fat required by these salmon to complete the long journey makes their flesh very desirable.

Jack salmon are young kings that have matured sexually after a year at sea, although the spawning age is normally from two to seven years.

During spawning, the king changes from a bright silver color to a dark red, in some cases so dark as to appear black.

Adult kings are characterized by black, irregular spots on the back and dorsal fins, and both lobes of the tail fin. The gum line is black also.

The size may vary to a great degree, with a three-year-old king weighing less than four pounds, and a mature seven-year-old exceeding 50 pounds.

King salmon, like all other members of the Pacific salmon family, hatch in fresh water, spend part of their life in the ocean, returning to fresh water to spawn, and then their life cycle ends.

Normally they are a bottom feeder and will hit egg clusters, most lures, bright spinners, and oakie drifters. Specific bait information is listed for different locations in the calendar of spawning runs section of this book.

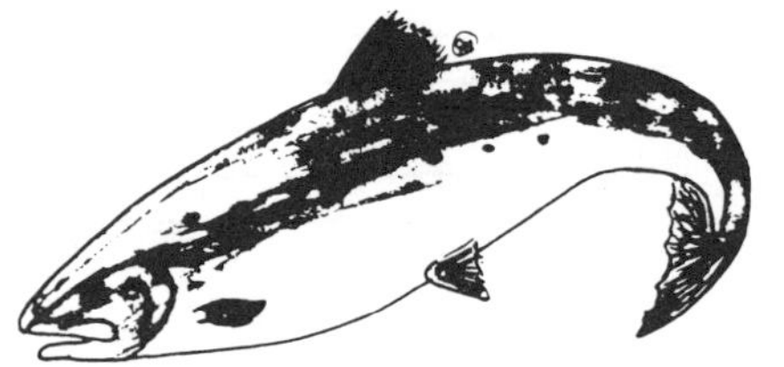

CALENDAR OF SALMON RUNS

Please Note: Dates given in the calendar are times of abundance, *not* Fish and Game Dept. open season dates—unless otherwise noted.

KING SALMON

** Note--All king salmon rivers and streams are subject to emergency closure or change. Check with the Department of Fish and Game for current regulations. Dates given are for the 1983 season.

★ SAT., SUN. & MONDAY'S ONLY. ★★ WEEK END FISHING ONLY.

UPPER COOK INLET

* Bait: Lures, spinners, oakie drifters, and egg clusters.

Deshka River—from its mouth upstream to Moose & Kroto Creek ______ Jan. 1st through July 6th
Alexander Creek ______ Jan. 1st through July 6th
Lake Creek (empties into the Yentna River) ______ Jan. 1st through July 6th
Clear Creek, tributary of the Talkeetna River (Also called Chunilna Creek.) ______ Jan. 1st through July 6th
The above creeks are accessible only by floatplane or riverboat.
Willow Creek—from its mouth upstream to Parks Highway ______ ★★ June 11th through July 3rd
Montana Creek—from its mouth upstream to Parks Highway ______ ★★ June 11th through July 3rd
Casell Creek—same as above ______ ★★ June 11th through July 3rd

KENAI PENINSULA

* Bait: Egg clusters and fluorescent 'Tee' spoons are favored. Assorted spoons and spinners are also effective.

Anchor River ______ ★ May 28th through June 20th
Deep Creek ______ ★ May 28th through June 20th
Kasilof River ______ Jan. 1st through June 30th
Ninilchik River ______ ★ May 28th through June 20th
Kenai River ______ Jan. 1st through July 31st
There are two king runs on the Kenai River in this time period. The second run of salmon are much larger fish, ranging from 50 to 80 pounds.

KING SALMON (Continued)

KODIAK ISLAND

Most waters open to King Salmon Fishing the entire year

* Bait: Egg clusters, fluorescent spoons, spinners and wet flies.

Karluk River ______ Runs begin in early June.
Fishing in the upper reaches of the river isn't good until the last week in June. By July 4th, 90% of the kings will be in the river. Spawning peaks in mid-August.

BRISTOL BAY

* Bait: Egg clusters, spinners, wet flies, and fluorescent spoons.

Naknek River, near King Salmon—certain sections restricted to use of fresh eggs ______ June 8th through April 9th
Nushagak River, upstream from the village of Portage Creek ______ June 8th through April 9th
Alagnak (Branch) River ______ June 8th through April 9th

FAIRBANKS AND NORTHERN ALASKA

* Bait: Egg clusters, spinners, wet flies, and fluorescent spoons.

Coastal areas ______ May 1st to July 30th.
Interior areas ______ July 1st to August 1st. Peaks July 15th.

COPPER RIVER-PRINCE WILLIAM SOUND

* Bait: Salmon egg clusters, fluorescent 'Tee' spoons, wet flies.

Gulkana River downstream from confulence of the middle fork ______ Peaks June and July.
Klutina River from outlet of Klutina Lake to marker 1 mile downstream ______ Peaks June and July.
Copper River ______ June and July, for possible dip netting.
Dip netting has been allowed in the past, during June and July. Check with the Department of Fish and Game for current regulations.

SOUTHEASTERN ALASKA

** Fresh water king salmon fishing is prohibited in this region. (From Dixon entrance to Cape Fairweather.)
Salt water king fishing is permitted.

MILLERS RIVER BOAT
SERVICE
OWNER:
TOM MAUSOLF
CHARTERS FOR:
KINGS • REDS • SILVERS
and TROUT
LITTLE SU AND DESHKA RIVERS
P.O. BOX 1, HOUSTON, ALASKA, 99694
(907) 892-6872 or 243-7350

SILVER SALMON

(Also called Cohoe, or Silverside)

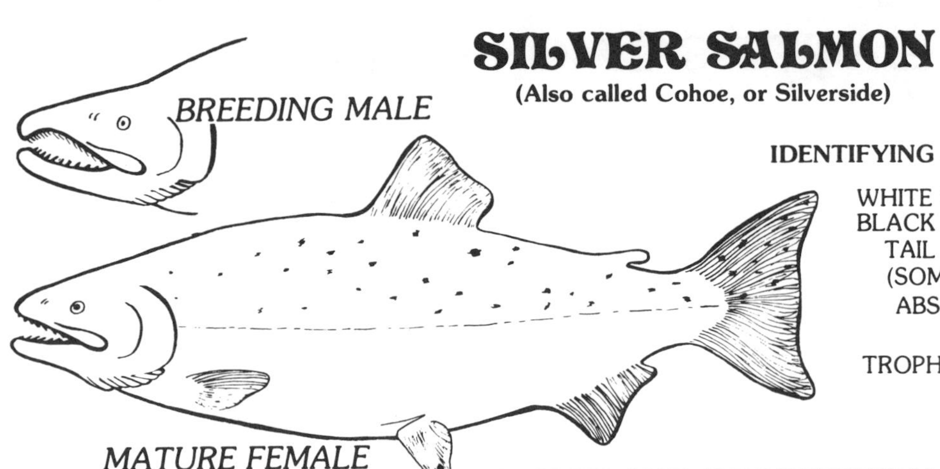

IDENTIFYING CHARACTERISTICS:

WHITE GUM LINE
BLACK SPOTS ON BACK AND UPPER LOBE OF TAIL
(SOMETIMES SPOTS ARE COMPLETELY ABSENT ON TAIL)

TROPHY SIZE - 18 pounds plus

RANGE AND DESCRIPTION

Ounce for ounce, the silver is probably the scrappiest fighter of the Pacific salmon family. In Alaskan waters, it ranges from Point Hope on the north to Southeastern Alaska, with migratory runs traveling far inland up the Yukon and Kuskokwim drainages. North of Norton Sound, the cohoe is not found in any numbers.

The current sports tackle record is a mighty 26-pounder, taken in Icy Straits in 1976 by Andrew A. Robbins. Nine to thirteen pounds is considered an average weight for silvers, and it has been noted that some runs contain consistently heavier fish, according to which stream the run is in.

The silver salmon will spawn in smaller streams than the king, and differs in the length of time it remains in fresh water before spawning. Usually, this is less than two weeks.

A dark red or brownish color is common for the silver when it has matured sexually and returned to its home stream for the spawning run.

Cohoes are a fall run salmon, not appearing in inland waters until late July and becoming more numerous in August, tapering off in September and October. Some streams have a later silver run, peaking in September.

The Cohoe is taken in salt and fresh water, and is not the finicky feeder that the red salmon is. They have a voracious appetite and will hit most any lure or bait.

CALENDAR OF SALMON RUNS (Continued)

SILVER SALMON

UPPER COOK INLET

* Bait: Salmon egg clusters, 'Tee' spoons, and Mepps spinners.

West side tributaries of the Susitna River.

Deshka River ____ Mid-July to September, peaks in August.
Lake Creek ____ Mid-July to September, peaks in August.
Alexander Creek ____ Mid-July to September, peaks in August.
Talachulitna River _ (unbaited, single-hook artifical lures only) ____ Mid-July to September, peaks in August.
Chuit River ____ Mid-July to September, peaks in August.
Quig Creek ____ Mid-July to September, peaks in August.
The above streams are accessible only by floatplane or riverboat.

East side tributaries of the Susitna River.

Little Susitna River ____ June 15th through April 14th - peaks from August 1st to September 15th.
This river supports the largest silver run in Upper Cook Inlet, approximately 10,000 salmon.
Sheep Creek ____ July 7th through May 31st - peaks from August 1st to September 15th.
Montana Creek ____ July 7th through May 31st - peaks from August 1st to September 15th.
Willow Creek ____ July 7th through May 31st - peaks from August 1st to September 15th.
Sunshine Creek ____ July 7th through May 31st - peaks from August 1st to September 15th.
Caswell Creek ____ July 7th through May 31st - peaks from August 1st to September 15th.
Wasilla, Cottonwood and Fish Creek _ Weekend fishing only ____ June 15th through April 14th

COPPER RIVER AREA

* Bait: Egg clusters, spoons and spinners.

Eyak River ____ Oct. 2nd through May 31st
Other streams along the Copper River Highway ____ (where not subject to closure) August and September.

CALENDAR OF SALMON RUNS (continued)

KENAI PENINSULA

★ Bait: Salmon egg clusters in glacial waters--Bright spoons, spinners, and streamer flies in clear water.
★ Sat. Sun. Monday only.

Kenai River — Late July to October.
This river has two peak seasons, occuring in early August and again in early September. Excellent fishing.

Anchor River — ★ May 28th through June 20th & July 1st through Apr. 14th
Ninilchik River — ★ May 28th through June 20th & July 1st through Apr. 14th
Deep Creek — ★ May 28th through June 20th & July 1st through Apr. 14th
Russian River — June 1st through Apr. 14th in designated areas

KODIAK ISLAND

★ Bait: Salmon clusters and lures.

Buskin River (Up to 12 pounds) — Sept. 11th through July 31st. Peaks in September.
American River — Late August into October. Peaks in September.
Saltery River and Pasagshak Rivers — (Daily Limit 2 Cohoe) — September through November. Peaks in September.
Karluk River — Spring season. Fall season, peaking in mid-August.
Afognak River — Lake August into October. Peaks in September.

BRISTOL BAY

★Bait Egg clusters or favored lures such as Golf-Tees.

Naknek River (north of King Salmon Creek) — closed from Apr. 10th through June 7th. Peaks in late July to mid-September.
Alagnak (Branch) River — Late July to mid-September.
Iguigig area (in the Kvichak watershed) — closed from Apr. 10th through June 7th) Special regulations this area.
Nushagak River (upstream from the village of Portage Creek) — Late July to mid-September.
Ugashik system, at the Narrows — Late July to mid-September.
Outlet of Lower Ugashik Lake — Late July to mid-September.
Mother Goose Lake — Late July to mid-September.

SOUTHEASTERN ALASKA

★Bait: Bright spoons and flies are favored in this area.

Port Banks on Baranof Island — August to early November. Peaks in September.
Situk River at Yakutat—from Old RR Bridge to U.S. Forest Sv. Middle Cabin — August to early November. Peaks in September.
Italio River Yakutat — August to early November. Peaks in September.

RED SALMON

IDENTIFYING CHARACTERISTICS:

NO SIZABLE SPOTS
(SOMETIMES HAS A DUSTING OF TINY SPECKS, LIKE PEPPER)
TURNS A BRIGHT RED, WITH A DEEP GREEN HEAD PRIOR TO SPAWNING

TROPHY SIZE - 10 pounds plus.

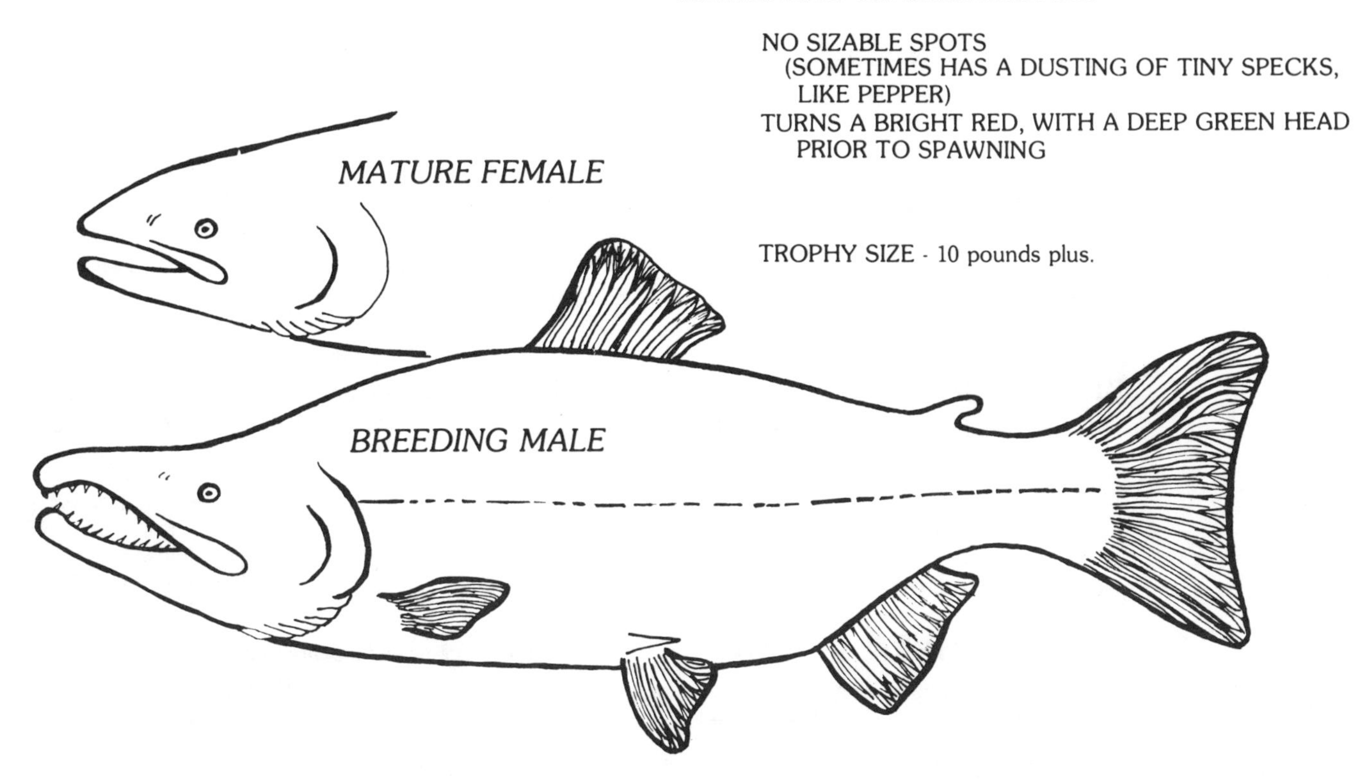

RED SALMON

(Also called sockeye and blueback.)

RANGE AND DESCRIPTION

The blueback, with its rich, bright red flesh, is the most valued of the smaller Pacific salmon. It rates very high in commercial importance.

The range of the red salmon reaches from Southeastern Alaska, north to the Seward Peninsula. It is even found in sparse numbers as far north as Point Hope. Inland, the sockeye extends as far as the mouth of the Koyukuk River and migrates up the Kuskokwim River and the streams along the Alaskan coast.

The average weight of the red is between six and 12 pounds. While in salt-water, it is a blueish silver, with the back a deep iridescent blue color. During spawning run the sockeye turns varying shades of red, sometimes a brilliant crimson. The head remains a dark green color.

In recent years, the red salmon has become recognized by sports fishermen as the fighting game fish it is. Not always is this salmon the aerial acrobat that the silver is, but it is a swift and powerful fighter. The secret is getting the sockeye to bite, because it is a moody, unpredictable fish. For years, it was believed that red salmon wouldn't hit a lure during the spawning run. Even now, techniques and lures that work well in one stream system will fail in another. Consistently, wet flies bring results in Brooks Lake in the Katmai Monument. And when the right pattern wet fly is used in the Russian River on the Kenai Peninsula, the fisherman is rewarded with excellent sport.

When fishing the Little Susitna River at the mouth of Lake Creek in the Upper Cook Inlet drainage system, I have had many reds bite on fresh eggs.

So, it really is a challenge to try to out-think the red salmon, and isn't that the name of the game.

The current sports record for sockeye in Alaska is a 16-pound fish caught in the Kenai River in 1974 by Chuck Leach.

Landlocked reds are called *kokanee*. They mature in lakes and do not return to sea. The size is much smaller that that of their sea-going cousins, normally not exceeding 16 inches in length in Alaskan waters.

Remember, the reds are a bottom feeder.

CALENDAR OF SALMON RUNS (Continued)

RED SALMON

UPPER COOK INLET

* Bait: Bright spoons and spinners, occasionally egg clusters

Little Susitna River —— peaks from July 10th to mid-August
Fish Creek ——
Clear Creek (tributary of the Talkeetna River) —— Late July to mid-August
Cottonwood Creek ——

KENAI PENINSULA

* Bait: Bright colored streamer flies.

Russian River —— Early June to late August

This river supports two red salmon runs--June 10th to July 1st, and July 10th to August 1st.

Kenai River —— Early June to late August.

The mouths of smaller tributaries flowing into this river

Moose River —— (special regulations in this area) Early June into September.

Fly fishing only in the Russian and Moose Rivers.

KODIAK ISLAND

* Bait: Streamer flies and small lures.

Afognak River —— June.
Uganik River —— June.
Buskin River —— Open Sept. 11 through July 31
Saltery River —— June.
Karluk River —— Early June into September.

CALENDAR OF SALMON RUNS (Continued)

RED SALMON (Continued)

BRISTOL BAY

* Bait: Streamer flies.

Brooks River in the Naknek River system_____ Late June and early July. (Fly fishing.)

COPPER RIVER-PRINCE WILLIAM SOUND

* Bait: Streamer flies.

Gulkana River_____ Closed above middle Fork/open season downstream from confluence. Late June and through July.
Klutina River_____ Late June and month of July.

PINK SALMON

(Also called humpback, or humpy.)

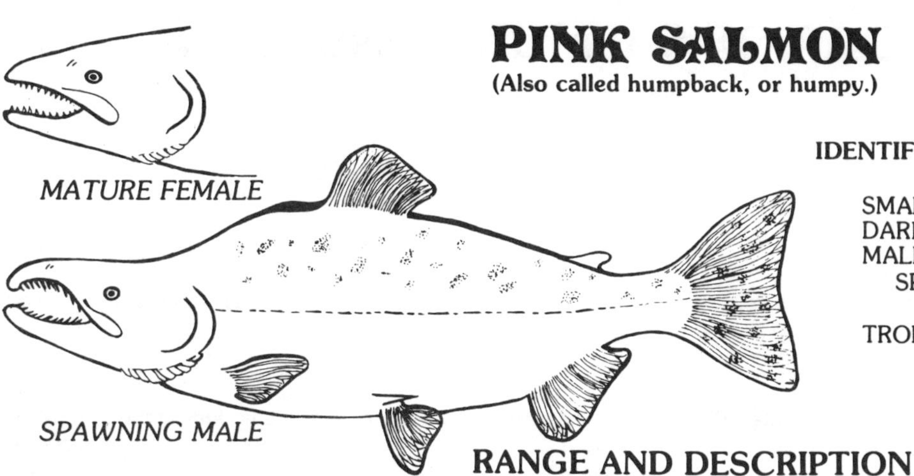

IDENTIFYING CHARACTERISTICS:

SMALL SCALES
DARK OVAL SPOTS ALONG BACK AND TAIL
MALES DEVELOP EXTREME HUMP DURING SPAWNING

TROPHY SIZE - 8 pounds plus.

RANGE AND DESCRIPTION

The pink is the smallest of the Pacific salmon, averaging three to five pounds. (Although catches of 10 pounds happen occasionally.) It is also the most abundant salmon in Alaskan waters during its peak alternate year. The pinks run in a two year cycle. This particular salmon species has an 'odd and even' year cycle. 1980 was a record peak year for humpies in the Upper Cook Inlet area, and most all of Alaska.

The sports tackle record in Alaska is a 12-pound, 9-ounce salmon caught by Steven Lee at Moose River in 1974.

Its range includes Southeastern Alaska, the Yakutat area, Prince William Sound, lower Kenai Peninsula north throughout the Susitna River drainage, the Kodiak-Afognak area, the entire Bristol Bay area, and north of the Seward Peninsula (coastal and inland).

The humpback is not considered the game fish that the king, silver and red salmon are. Its flesh is not as desirable for consumption because it lacks the firmness and bright red color.

Fresh-from-the-sea pinks put up a good fight on light tackle, but the males change rapidly after reaching fresh water. In a week or so, they begin to develop the grotesque hump on their back, and the extremely hooked jaw.

Pinks mature in two years and return to their home streams, beginning the spawning runs in July and continuing through September.

Salt and fresh water are both productive for humpies. Artificial lures are good, with bright shiny spoons, spinners, etc. bringing the best results.

CALENDAR OF SALMON RUNS (Continued)

PINK SALMON

UPPER COOK INLET

* Bait: Small daredevils are good, most of the small Mepps lures, also salmon egg clusters.

These salmon are so numerous in the Cook Inlet drainage system that almost any of the inland streams will produce pink salmon. Even year runs are always best for Pinks, odd numbered years poor.

Alexander and Lake Creeks and the Deshka River ________ July 10th to August 15th.
Clear Creek (tributary of the Talkeetna River) ________ July 20th to August 20th.
All streams and rivers crossed by the Parks Highway, from and including the
Little Susitna River to the Talkeetna River ________ (open June 15th through April 14th) peaks from July 15th to August 15th.

KENAI PENINSULA

* Bait: Same as above.

Kenai River (lower), below the Skilak Lake outlet ________ Late July through August.
Resurrection Creek (near Hope) ________ Late July through August.

These waters are two of the largest run locations.

KODIAK ISLAND

* Bait: Same as above.

All streams around Kodiak and Afognak Islands ________ Peak season-July and early August.

CALENDAR OF SALMON RUNS (Continued)

PINK SALMON (Continued)

BRISTOL BAY--COPPER RIVER-PRINCE WILLIAM SOUND--AND SOUTHEASTERN ALASKA

Generally the pink salmon is found throughout the entire state, and in such numbers that it would be difficult to find any sizable waterway that did not have a spawning run of these salmon.

July and August are the times of abundance in all waters for the pink salmon.

FAIRBANKS AND NORTHERN ALASKA

* Bait: Same as above.

Coastal streams only ________ June 15th to mid-August. Peaks in July.
Excellent fishing is to be had in the Unalakleet River on Norton Sound.
Also in the Nome, Snake and Nuikluk Rivers near Nome.

(907) 235-6687
Box 501
Homer, AK

FLY-IN FISHING and

SALMON & HALIBUT CUSTOM CHARTERS

Cruise beautiful Kachemak Bay and sample it's excellent sport fishing.

Bud & Audie Berryman

CHUM SALMON

(Also called *dog*, or calico.)

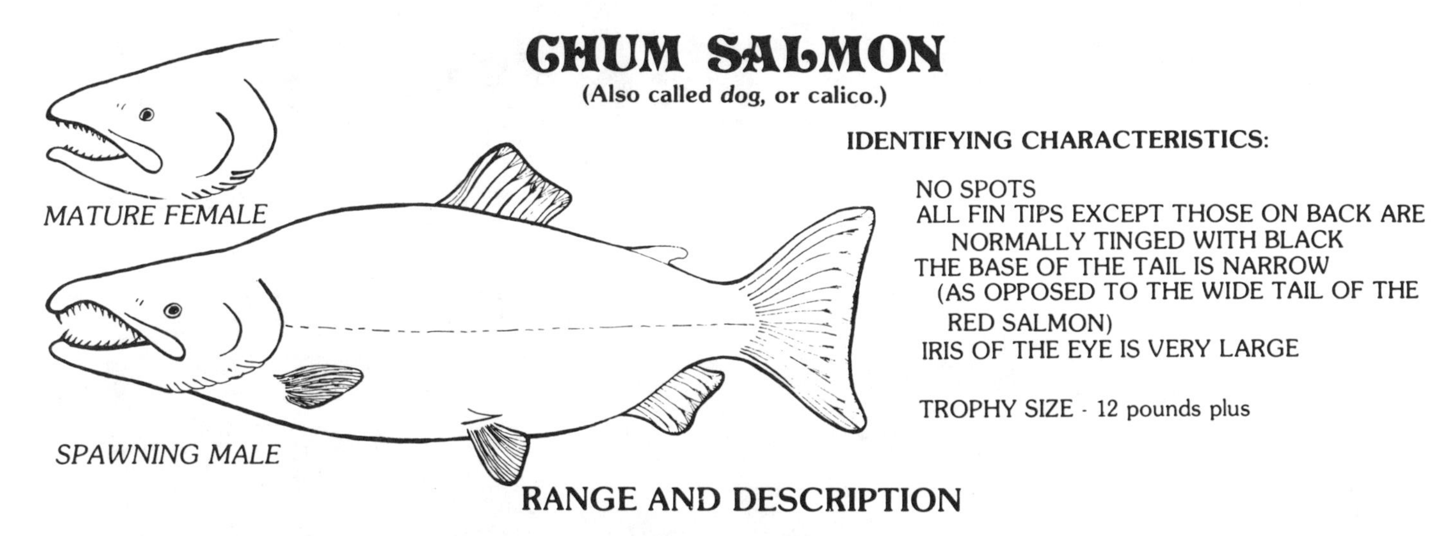

IDENTIFYING CHARACTERISTICS:

NO SPOTS
ALL FIN TIPS EXCEPT THOSE ON BACK ARE NORMALLY TINGED WITH BLACK
THE BASE OF THE TAIL IS NARROW (AS OPPOSED TO THE WIDE TAIL OF THE RED SALMON)
IRIS OF THE EYE IS VERY LARGE

TROPHY SIZE - 12 pounds plus

RANGE AND DESCRIPTION

Chum salmon range further north than any other species of the Pacific salmon. They are commonly found in Kotzebue Sound, migrating (in sparse numbers) on to the Mackenzie River area in Arctic Canada.

The chum is found in Southeastern Alaska and along the Alaska mainland in coastal streams, seldom moving further inland than 100 miles. (With the exception of the longer Kuskokwim and Yukon River runs.)

The average weight for the dog salmon is from nine to 10 pounds. Forty-pound chums have been reported as being caught, but there is no official record of this. The record fish caught in Alaska on sports tackle was a 27-pound, 3-ounce salmon, landed by Robert Jahnke at Behm Canal in 1977.

Spawning males and females develop barred coloration along the side, with dark vertical bars and colors of black, gray and in later stages, a reddish pink and yellow. From these colors came the nickname *calico*.

The male's nose becomes sharply hooked and the teeth exposed, resembling a dog's fangs.

The chum is the least popular of the five Pacific salmon to Alaskan anglers. Not a good feeder, this salmon will seldom hit a lure or bait in either fresh or salt water. At times, if a bright shiny spoon or spinner is presented to them often enough, they may strike out of annoyance.

CHUM SALMON

UPPER COOK INLET

* Bait: Chums will hit any lure or bait used for silver. They tend not to feed during the spawning run, (similar in this respect to the red salmon). They are a fall run salmon.

Chum salmon aren't found in the numbers that silvers, reds and humpys are in inland waters.

Try Willow, Alexander, Montana and Caswell Creeks.

FAIRBANKS AND NORTHERN ALASKA

* Bait: Same as above.

Interior waters ____ August 15th to November 1st, peaks in September.
Coastal waters ____ July 15th to September 30th, peaks in September.
Fishing is excellent during mid-July on the lower Nome and Niukluk Rivers.

STEELHEAD

RANGE AND DESCRIPTION

The classification of this fabled fighting fish was controversial for many years. It is now accepted that it is the sea-run species of the Rainbow trout.

The color phase of the steelhead varies greatly. Returning from the sea, this fish is a silvery color, blue-gray along the back, and white on the belly. Fresh water brings the rosy band of color on the sides back into view, along with the black spots covering the back,sides, and tail.

Three of Alaska's regions support the steelhead. Southeastern, the Kenai Peninsula, and Kodiak Island.

In Southeastern Alaska, there are two separate runs of this trophy fish. One occurs during September, October and early November in lower Southeastern, and on the Situk River near Yakutat in October and November.

The second run is in the spring, and enters the larger streams throughout Southeastern in April, peaking in May.

Salmon eggs are the preferred bait in this locality, next in popularity are spoons, then flies.

Kenai Peninsula steelhead waters are as follows: Anchor River, Deep Creek, and the Ninilchik River. Favored bait and lures are: salmon eggs, spin'n glows, and okie drifters. Fluorescent flies work well also. Steelhead runs enter the above named fresh water streams in August, September and October, and the trout may winter in fresh water, returning to salt water in late spring.

Fishing peaks on Kodiak Island in October in the Karluk, Frazer, Aykelik, (Red River) and Saltery Rivers.

Fishing is best for steelhead when water temperatures are above 40 degrees. A wary, spooky fish, the steelhead must be lured gently to strike bait or lures. Drifting salmon eggs or a streamer fly on, or near the bottom is usually the most effective method to use.

These fighting fish lie up in deep waterholes upstream or downstream from long, shallow stretches. The area of a stream just above or below rapids is normally also productive. Cast upstream and allow bait or fly to sink and bounce along the bottom, where the steelhead are.

Approved tackle to use would be a limber seven to nine foot rod, 10-pound test leaders with monofilament line of the same test for spin fishing.

The current steelhead state record is a mighty 42-pounder, landed by David White in 1970 at Bell Island.

SPORTS FISH CALENDAR

STEELHEAD

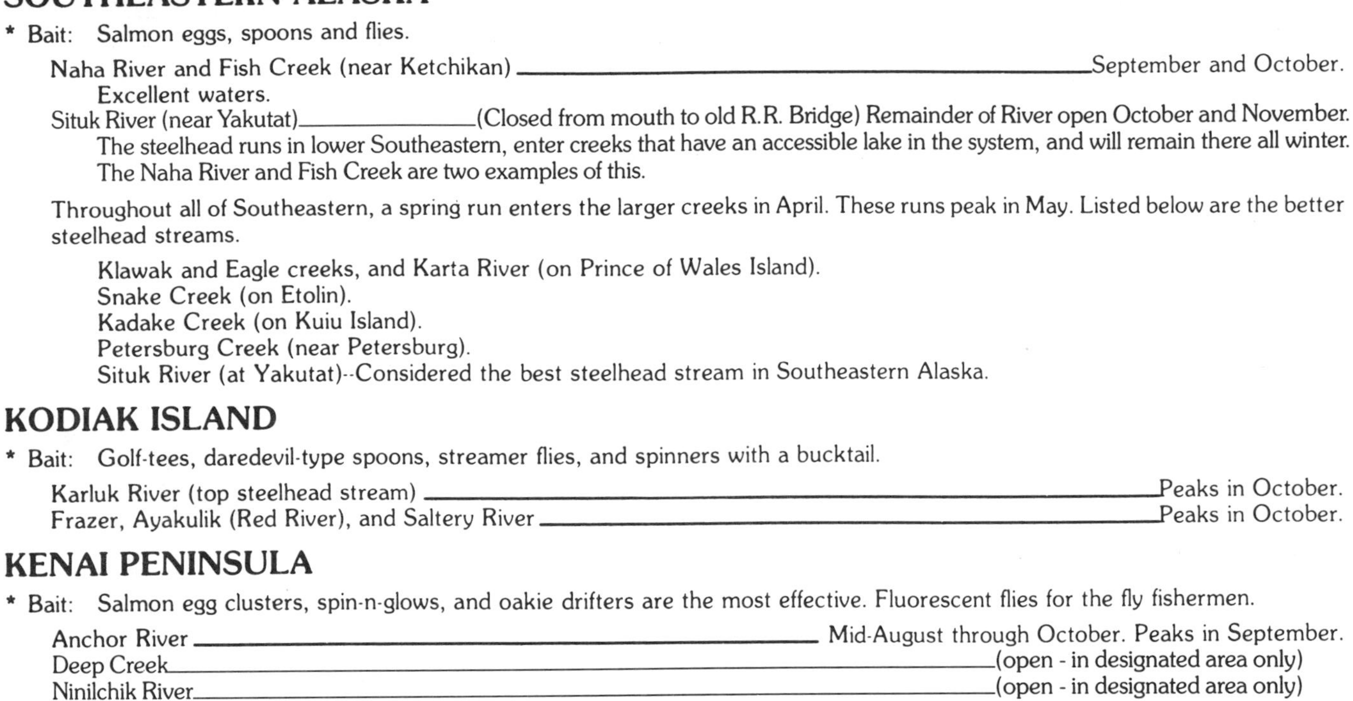

SOUTHEASTERN ALASKA

* Bait: Salmon eggs, spoons and flies.

Naha River and Fish Creek (near Ketchikan) — September and October.
Excellent waters.

Situk River (near Yakutat) — (Closed from mouth to old R.R. Bridge) Remainder of River open October and November.
The steelhead runs in lower Southeastern, enter creeks that have an accessible lake in the system, and will remain there all winter. The Naha River and Fish Creek are two examples of this.

Throughout all of Southeastern, a spring run enters the larger creeks in April. These runs peak in May. Listed below are the better steelhead streams.

Klawak and Eagle creeks, and Karta River (on Prince of Wales Island).
Snake Creek (on Etolin).
Kadake Creek (on Kuiu Island).
Petersburg Creek (near Petersburg).
Situk River (at Yakutat)--Considered the best steelhead stream in Southeastern Alaska.

KODIAK ISLAND

* Bait: Golf-tees, daredevil-type spoons, streamer flies, and spinners with a bucktail.

Karluk River (top steelhead stream) — Peaks in October.
Frazer, Ayakulik (Red River), and Saltery River — Peaks in October.

KENAI PENINSULA

* Bait: Salmon egg clusters, spin-n-glows, and oakie drifters are the most effective. Fluorescent flies for the fly fishermen.

Anchor River — Mid-August through October. Peaks in September.
Deep Creek — (open - in designated area only)
Ninilchik River — (open - in designated area only)

RAINBOW TROUT

RANGE AND DESCRIPTION

This well known member of the trout family is aptly named. It is marked with a rosy band of color from gill cover to tail along its midsection. Black spots are scattered along the dark-colored back, fading to a silvery white on the belly.

The distribution of the rainbow places it as far north as Stony River, a tributary of the Kuskokwim River in Alaska. Kodiak Island, the Upper Cook Inlet drainage, Kenai Peninsula, Prince William Sound, the Yakutat area, and Southeastern Alaska are all home waters to this chunky, battling trout. The clearwater lakes and streams draining into Bristol Bay produce rainbow trout in greater numbers, and of a larger size than any other area of the state.

The top rainbow waters are the Wood River Lakes and the Naknek and Kvichak drainages in Bristol Bay. Brooks River in Katmai National Monument has long been known for its trophy rainbows.

These sports fish are more active when the temperature is above 40 degrees, so fishing is best during late spring, summer and fall. A hungry eater, the fresh-water rainbow is not particular about his diet. Fresh eggs, lures, spoons, and flies are all good.

Many sports fishermen believe the wobbling spoon is a sure-fire rainbow-getter, while a dyed-in-the-wool fly fisherman swears by streamer flies and modified bucktails fished near the bottom. Black and red combinations work well. If the angler prefers lures, try silver and fluorescent red.

Be sure to fish the bottom if you are after the big lunkers of ten pounds or so. Lures will be lost certainly, but 'faint heart never won fair game.'

The current State sports record was caught by David White in 1970 at Bell Island. It weighed a tremendous 42 pounds, two ounces.

Trophy-size rainbows, 12 pounds plus.

RAINBOW TROUT

UPPER COOK INLET

* Bait: Salmon egg clusters and spinning-type lures.

Deshka River — Late May until September 1st.
Alexander and Lake Creeks — Late May until September 1st.
Headwaters of the Deshka and Peters Creek — Late May until September 1st.
Above streams accessible by floatplane or riverboat only.
Willow and Montana Creeks — July 7th through May 31st
East side tributaries of the Susitna River.
Bradley-Kepler Lake Complex, near Palmer — All year.
Matanuska, Knik, Wasilla, Big, and Lower Bonnie Lakes — All year.
Jewell, Campbell Point, Beach and Sand Lakes (Anchorage area) — All year.

KENAI PENINSULA

* Bait: Salmon egg clusters and spinning-type lures.

Swan Lake and Swanson River Canoe systems (Kenai National Moose Range) — Open June 15th through April 14th.
Upper Russian River and Russian Lakes — Open June 1st through April 14th in designated area.
Rainbows up to 24 inches.
Moose River and Swanson River drainages — Open June 15th through April 14th.
Cabin Lake, in North Kenai — All year.
Jerome Lake, north of Moose Pass — All year.
Johnson and Longmare Lakes, Soldotna area — All year.

(Continued)

SPORTS FISH CALENDAR (Continued)

RAINBOW TROUT (Continued)

KODIAK ISLAND

★ Bait: Salmon egg clusters and spinning-type lures.

Bell's Flat Lakes, Cliff Point Lakes, Woody Island Lakes ____________ All year.
Pasagshak Point Lakes ____________ All year.

Rivers are best fished in early June.

Most river-lake systems offer good Rainbow Trout fishing on both Afognak and Kodiak Islands.

BRISTOL BAY

* Bait: Same as above.

The water system making up the Bristol Bay watershed affords the best Rainbow fishing in the entire state, with the exception of the Egegik and Ugashik Lakes systems.

Listed below are the most productive areas.

Kvichak drainage, including Iliamna Lake____________Open June 8 through Oct. 31, & Nov. 1 through April 9th
Naknek drainage____________Open June 8th through Apr. 9th

The above systems are closed to fishing from April 10th through June 7th to protect spawning trout.

Lower Talarik Creek____________September and October.
Newhalen, Iliamna and Gibraltor Rivers____________(Gibraltar open June 8th-Oct. 31st/&Nov. 1st-Apr. 9th)

With the exception of Lower Talarik Creek, the above listed waterways are best fished from late August to freeze-up.

★ Note--Unbaited single-hook artificials lures only may be used in the Kvichak watershed. June through Oct. 31.

COPPER RIVER-PRINCE WILLIAM SOUND

* Bait: Egg clusters, spoons, flies and shrimp.

Blueberry, Worthington, Sculpin, Buffalo, and Van Lakes ____________ Year round.

These are all roadside lakes.

RAINBOW TROUT (Continued)

FAIRBANKS AND NORTHERN ALASKA

* Bait: Salmon egg clusters and spinning-type lures.

Aniak River ________ Year round.
Kuskokwim River drainage ________ Year round.
Donna, Mark, Little Donna, Rapids, and Quartz Lakes (Delta Junction Area) ________ Year round.
16 to 22 inch Rainbows are common in Quartz Lake.
Rainbow Lake ________ Year round.
This lake affords excellent Rainbow fishing. It is located across the Tanana River from Big Delta, and is accessible only by floatplane during summer months, or by winter trail.

SOUTHEASTERN ALASKA

* Bait: Egg clusters, spoons, flies and shrimp.

Blue Lake, near Sitka ________ May through September.
Swan Lake, near Petersburg ________ May through September.
Walker Lake, near Ketchikan ________ May through September.
McDonald Lake, near Ketchikan ________ May through September.
Rezanof Lake and its water system, Baranof Island ________ May through September.

DOLLY VARDEN TROUT

RANGE AND DESCRIPTION

The Dolly is the most abundant of the trout family in Alaska. Its distribution occurs along the coastline from Southeastern Alaska to the Alaska Peninsula and the Aleutian Chain, extending through Bristol Bay and up the Arctic coastline into Canada. Large populations are found in interior waters.

These trout, like the salmon, migrate to the sea and return to fresh water to spawn. Spawning occurs from September to November. Not until the third or fourth year of life does the Dolly make its spring migration to the sea, where it will feed for two or three months, then return to a fresh water lake to winter. This feeding migration to the sea during summer months and return in the fall, to winter in fresh water, forms a pattern repeated each year.

While in salt water, the Dolly is a silvery color. In fresh water, it may turn a dark brown or black, with a bright red belly, white-rimmed belly fins and the distinguishing red or orange spots along the sides. The weight can reach 11 or 12 pounds. Salt water fishing for the Dolly Varden is best from May through July. These trout school up to feed along the shoreline, especially near sandy beaches that have a steep drop, or near fine-gravel beaches.

Fresh water coastal streams are good during August and September. Try fishing near spawning salmon, in deep holes, or at the mouth of a creek on an incoming tide.

Lake fishing for sea-run dollies is best from late August through November. Spring fishing brings best results using small spinning lures in lake outlet streams and in salt water. Spring and summer, use streamer flies along the saltwater beaches. August and September, try spinning lures or a single salmon egg bounced along the bottom. Wet and dry flies produce good results in either streams or lakes.

Dolly Varden are voracious feeders, and at one time or other, will hit most any bait, spoon, lure, spinner or fly offered.

The current Alaska State record is a 17-pound, eight-ounce Dolly taken at the Wulik River in 1968 by Peter Winslow.

Trophy-size Dolly Varden, 10 pounds plus.

DOLLY VARDEN TROUT

UPPER COOK INLET

* Bait: Salmon eggs, brightly colored lead-head jigs, and small spinning lures.

Lewis River and Coal Creek (near Coal Creek Lake, northwest of Tyonek) ____ Year round.
Theodore, Chuit and Talachulitna Rivers ____ Year round.

Dollies are not overly abundant in this region. During salmon spawning runs in the fall they will follow the salmon up rivers and streams into interior lakes such as Big Lake. The Dolly is stocked by the Department of Fish and Game in some of the lakes in the Kepler Lakes Complex (near Palmer).

KENAI PENINSULA

* Bait: Salmon eggs, wet flies or nymphs and small bright lures.

Anchor River ____ **July 1st through Apr. 14th**
Ninilchik River ____ **July 1st through Apr. 14th**
Deep Creek ____ **July 1st through April 14th**
Quartz Creek ____ **July 1st through April 14th**
Ptarmigan Creek ____ July through November.
Kenai River ____ July through November.

This river is a good bet for 'lunker' Dolly Varden.

Upper and Lower Summit Lakes (and connecting water system) afford fishing for a small, landlocked variety called 'goldenfins'. They are found in two other lakes on the Kenai Peninsula: Jerome Lake near Moose Pass, and Grouse Lake near Seward.

SPORTS FISH CALENDAR (Continued)

DOLLY VARDEN (Continued)

KODIAK ISLAND

* Bait: Salmon eggs, wet flies and small lures.

Bushkin River ______ During spring-May. During fall-September.
Afognak River ______ During spring-May. During fall-September.
Saltery River ______ During spring-May. During fall-September.
Pasagshak River ______ During spring-May. During fall-September.

These trout occur in large numbers in streams throughout the island. Listed above are the most popular spots.

FAIRBANKS AND NORTHERN ALASKA

* Bait: Same as above.

Sinuk River, near Nome ______ August and September.

This river offers exceptional Dolly fishing.

Wulik River, Kivalina area ______ August and September.
Nenana River, near Nenana ______ Right after spring break-up.
Tanana River, near the Johnson River confluence ______ Right after spring break-up.
Try the tributaries of the Nenana and Tanana Rivers.
Coastal streams are productive for the entire season.

SOUTHEASTERN ALASKA

* Bait: Salmon eggs, flies, spoons.

Trout of up to seven pounds are caught in this region of Alaska.

Situk River (Yakutat River system) ______ Year round, best from late August through September.
Hasselborg Lake - Juneau area ______ Year round, best from late August through September.
Thayer Lake - Juneau area ______ Year round, best from late August through September.
Turner Lake - Juneau area ______ Year round, best from late August through September.
Chilkat Lake, Haines area ______ Year round, best from late August through September.

SOUTHEASTERN ALASKA (Continued)

Goulding Lakes, Chichagof Island — Year round, best from late August through September.
Petersburg Lake, near Petersburg — Year round, best from late August through September.
Stikine River, (Wrangell area) — Year round, best from late August through September.
Virginia, Martin and Kunk Lakes (Wrangell area) — Year round, best from late August through September.
Unuk, Karta and Naha Rivers (Ketchikan area) — Year round, best from late August through September.
Humpback, Ella, Wilson and Manzanita Lakes (Ketchikan area) — Same time frame as above.

MIGRATORY TROUT

* Bait: Salmon eggs, flies, spoons.

Chilkoot Lake (Haines area) — April to early June; late July to November.
Nakwasina and Katlian Rivers (Sitka area) — April to early June; late July to November.
Duncan Canal, Saltchuck and Castle River (In the Petersburg area) — April to early June; late July to November.
Salmon Bay Creek — April to early June; late July to November.
Bostwick Inlet and Wasta Creek — April to early June; late July to November.

COPPER RIVER-PRINCE WILLIAM SOUND

* Bait: Salmon eggs, spoons, lures.

Streams near Valdez and Cordova provide the best Dolly fishing.

LAKE TROUT

(Also called Mackinaw, Togue,and Great Lakes Trout.)

RANGE AND DESCRIPTION

Alaska's largest freshwater fish is also the largest of the group of fishes known as char. The Laker is common in Bristol Bay lakes, in drainages north of Cook Inlet, and in interior Alaska north of the Brooks Range (excluding the North Slope lowlands). The Kobuk drainage contains good lake trout fishing, although lakers are not found within 400 miles of the Bering Straits.

In appearance, their body shape is common to that of other trout and salmon. Color phases vary greatly during different seasons and different localitites. The basic color can be from very dark to a pale gray, while the spots are light in color and irregularly shaped. One distinguishing characteristic of the lake trout is the deeply forked tail.

The laker is a deep, cold-water trout. It spawns normally in early fall, when the temperature cools to 50 degrees. Most lake trout live and die in the same lake, and they are the least migratory of the trout family.

It is a large -mouthed fish and feeds heavily on whitefish, lake herring, smelt, grayling, arctic char and stickle-backs. A bait that resembles a wounded fish will sometimes work when other baits have failed.

Try fishing lake inlets during summer months and into fall. Lakers can be found here feeding on forage fish and insects carried in by the current.

Trolling is usually the most productive method to use, especially in summer months. The laker prefers the colder temperatures and stays deep, except for the short period of time after ice break-up. It then moves near the surface and will feed on almost anything.

During this period, flies, streamers, and bucktails are productive. Spin fishing, using shiny lures such as spoons, wobblers or spinners reward the angler well. Remember, as the the temperature rises, the lake trout go deeper, so fish accordingly.

The record lake trout caught on sports tackle in Alaska was a 47-pounder taken in Clarence Lake by Daniel Thorsness in July of 1970. This mighty trout measured 44½ inches. A 102-pound monster was taken from Athabasca Lake in Canada and still stands as the world's record.

Easily accessible laker waters are Summit and Paxson Lakes off the Richardson Highway. Clarence and Crosswind Lakes, and the Lake Louise complex off the Glenn Highway are the waters to fish if you're looking for lunkers. For a numerous catch, not trophy-size lake trout, try the Bristol Bay region. Inlet streams into Lake Clark, Naknek Lake, or the outlet of the Tikchik Lakes are all excellent spots.

Trophy-size Lake trout, 20 pounds plus.

LAKE TROUT (Continued)

UPPER COOK INLET

* Bait: Medium-sized red and white spoons and blue-tinted minnow-type lures, trolled at 30 feet depth minimum.

Shell Lake (Skwentna area) — Summer season.
This is a fly-in area. A small motor-propelled raft is needed for trolling.

KENAI PENINSULA

* Bait: Generally, lakers will take most baits that resemble a wounded fish. Right after break-up, flat-wing flies, bucktails and streamers are usually good. If spin fishing, try spoons, spinners or wobblers; gold or silver colored are most effective.

Kenai River system, all glacial lakes — All season, best right after break-up and just before freezing.
Skilak Lake, inlet and outlet — All season, best right after break-up and again just before freezing.
Tustemena Lake, outlet — All season, best right after break-up and again just before freezing.
Resurrection Pass Trail System — All season, best after break-up and just before freezing.
Mountain lakes accessible by trail.
Hidden Lake — All season, best right after break-up and again just before freezing.
Good when the shallow waters are trolled using spoons or flatfish. Winter ice fishing is usually productive. Try jigging with spoons under the ice.

BRISTOL BAY

* Bait: Same as for Kenai Peninsula.

This region offers the best lake trout fishing in Alaska.

Tikchik Lakes, outlets — All season, best right after break-up and again just before freezing.
Lake Clark, inlet streams — Same as above.

(Continued)

SPORTS FISH CALENDAR (Continued)

BRISTOL BAY (Continued)

Battle River ______ Same time schedule as Tikchik Lakes.
Nonvianuk Lake ______ Same as above.
Naknek Lake ______ Same as above.

FAIRBANKS AND NORTHERN ALASKA

* Bait: Same as for the Kenai Peninsula.

Brooks Range Area:

Shainin, Chandler, Kurupa, Elusive and Itkillik Lakes, on the North Slope.
Selby-Harvak, Wild, Helpmejack, Chandalar, Squaw and Walker Lakes on the South Slope.

The above named lakes are best fished right after break-up and again just before freeze-up.

Fielding and Tangle Lakes, Paxson area ______ Same as above.
Monte Lake, Robertson River area ______ Same as above.
Harding Lake, near Fairbanks ______ Same as above.

A small number of lakers have been stocked in this lake.

COPPER RIVER-PRINCE WILLIAM SOUND

* Bait: Spoons, red-eyes, or Alaskan plugs.

Right after break-up in the spring, and just before freezing are the best times to fish. During summer months, when the water warms, try deep trolling.

Crosswind, Clarence, Susitna, Beaver, Dog, Paxson, Summit, Swede, Tanada and Copper Lakes, Lake Louise. All are off the Glenn Highway.

Several of the small lakes along the Denali Highway afford good 'Laker' fishing for the shore angler.

SHEEP CREEK LODGE
MILE 88.2 PARKS HIGHWAY
(907) 495-6227
RUSTIC CABINS FOR LODGING
GOOD FISHING
GOOD FOOD
WARM, HAPPY ALASKAN ATMOSPHERE

CUTTHROAT TROUT

RANGE AND DESCRIPTION

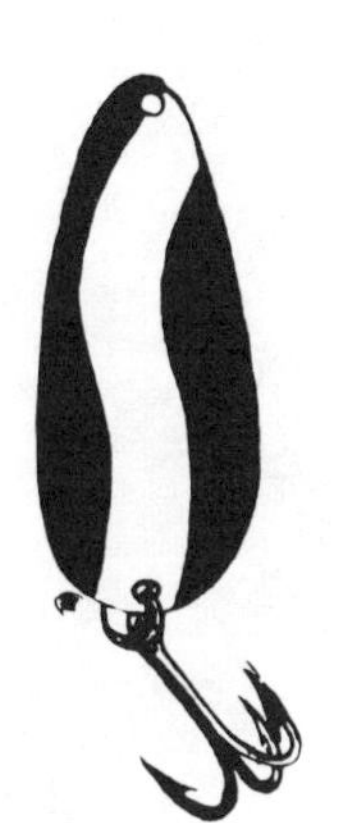

The cutthroat trout is found in one of the seven major fishing divisions in Alaska. It is common throughout Southeastern Alaska, ranging north as far as Montague Island in Prince William Sound.

This trout is named for the two red streaks of color usually visible under the chin. Like the Dolly Varden, some cutthroat migrate to sea and return to spawn in fresh water streams.

While in salt water, the cutthroat is a silver color, with the numerous black spots of the body, tail and fins barely visible; likewise, the twin red marks under the chin.

In fresh water, it turns a dark blue-green over the back, becoming a pinkish-purple color along the sides, fading to a light-colored belly. The spots and red markings are pronounced in this stage.

Sea-run cutthroat may reach a weight of 6 pounds, although weights from one to four pounds are average.

An eight-pound, six-ounce trout is the current state record. It was taken from Wilson Lake in 1977 by Robert Denison.

Saltwater fishing is best in inlets and shallow bays along the coastline. Try at high tide, early mornings or evenings. Stream mouths, where natural feed such as small salt and fresh water fish congregate are good spots.

Fresh water fishing is best in the deep lakes of Southeastern. Cutthroat stay in the shallow areas of these lakes, feeding near stream mouths.

Trophy-size Cutthroat trout, 3 pounds plus.

EASTERN BROOK TROUT

RANGE AND DESCRIPTION

The Eastern Brook is another member of the trout family found only in Southeastern waters. It was introduced from the East Coast in the early 1900's. The brook trout flourished in the cold waters of the North, although never reaching the size of its Eastern relatives. Twelve to 15 inches is the maximum size caught in Alaska.

In color the Eastern Brook is very dark, of either a gray or greenish shade, and is marked with spots lighter than the background (of gray, white or red). These spots sometimes have a lighter color border, giving the effect of a small bullseye. The back and dorsal fin may have dark green wavy marks.

Trophy-size Eastern Brook trout, 3 pounds plus.

SOUTHEASTERN ALASKA

* Bait: Salmon eggs, spoons, flies and shrimp.

Salmon Creek Reservoir (Juneau area) ________ Year round.
Green and Thimbleberry Lakes (Sitka area) ________ Year round.
Grace and Perseverance Lakes (Ketchikan area) ________ Year round.

ARCTIC CHAR

RANGE AND DESCRIPTION

The Arctic Char inhabits coastal regions of the Alaska Peninsula, the Bering Straits, and the Arctic region. It is limited on the Kenai Peninsula to lakes in the Swanson River drainage. Most streams on the Seward Peninsula support char. The most productive fishing is in August and September, when the char follow the spawning salmon up the waterways.

The Kotzebue area is best fished in September. Trophy char can be caught in the Wulik and Kivalina Rivers, and the Noatuk and Kobuk River drainages. Some Arctic Char are found in the Tanana River tributaries near the Johnson River confluence and also in tributaries of the Nenana River near the town of Nenana. The prime time to fish these waters is immediately after breakup.

Isolated areas of the Brooks Range are included in the chars' native habitat, especially in coastal streams.

Wonder Lake in Mt. McKinley National Park contains this Arctic species, as do scattered localities in the Aleutian Islands.

The char, a close relative of the Dolly Varden trout, is a lake spawning fish. In appearance, it resembles the Dolly, but it is more brightly colored. The polka-dot orange or red spots are very vivid during spawning, and the belly of the male turns a crimson red. The pectoral and pelvic fins show a rim of white along the smooth line of the fins.

Spawning occurs every other year in September and October.

The state record is currently a 17-pound, 8-ounce lunker taken from the Wulik River near Kivlina by Peter Winslow in 1968. It measured 36 inches in length.

Salmon eggs, spoons and spinners have all proved effective for the char. Red and white spoons, or even better, a copper spoon with a red fluorescent stripe have proved most productive.

In summer months, the angler must troll deep for these cold-water fish, for as lake waters warm, the char will move to the bottom. Spring and fall still remain the best seasons for the angler to try his luck.

Trophy-size Arctic Char, 10 pounds plus.

ARCTIC CHAR

KENAI PENINSULA

* Bait: Salmon eggs, spoons and spinners.

Stormy, Finger, Fish and Dolly Varden Lakes — Deep trolling/summer months.

Many other lakes in the Swanson River and Swan Lake canoe systems will produce good char fishing.

Spring and fall fishing for the shore angler.

FAIRBANKS AND NORTHERN AREA

* Bait: Same as above.

Coastal streams — Available through the season.
Seward Peninsula streams — August and September.
Nenana River tributaries, Nenana area — All season.
Johnson River area, confluence with the Tanana River — All season.
Wulik and Kivalina Rivers — September fishing is best. Trophy size.
Tributaries of the Noatak River (Kotzebue area) — September fishing is best. Trophy size.

ARCTIC GRAYLING

RANGE AND DESCRIPTION

Grayling are the most widely distributed sport fish in Alaska. They can be found in all seven regions of the state. In 1962, grayling were introduced to Southeastern Alaska, where they adapted and increased in numbers and now provide excellent fishing.

Generally, it can be said that the grayling season is from the last of April through September, however, the best grayling fishing in the Copper River-Prince William Sound and Upper Cook Inlet systems occurs during May and June.

The Kenai Peninsula region has a limited distribution of these game fish, whereas Bristol Bay has an abundance. The record-breakers are found in the outlet of lower Ugashik Lake during July and August.

Fairbanks and the Northern Alaska region is best fished early and late in the season if the angler wants the larger grayling. The Norton Sound area supports lunkers in the Sinuk, Niuluk and Fish Rivers near Nome. Unalakeet River is good and so is the Nation River (downstream from Eagle).

The Arctic Grayling has a small, tender mouth, and it has that characteristic which makes it easy to identify: the high dorsal fin that resembles a sail. This fin is marked with bright spots of red and blue while in water. Depending on the home waters of the grayling, it will vary in color from very dark to a pearly shade.

An average length will run from 10 to 15 inches. Any grayling 20 inches or longer is trophy size. The present state record is a four-pound, 11-ounce fish taken from Ugashik Narrows in 1975 by Duane Weaver. The length was 21½ inches.

Small flies, shrimp, salmon eggs, and spinners are all effective for grayling. A general rule to remember is that salmon eggs are best during the spring months, when the water is high. Flies, especially the mosquito, brown and gray hackle, and small spinners will bring better results in summer and fall when the water clears. Grayling are a top water feeder.

Trophy-size Arctic grayling, 3 pounds plus.

ARCTIC GRAYLING

UPPER COOK INLET

* Bait: Salmon eggs during the spring months, or when water is high. Flies and small spinners during the summer and fall months.

Deshka River and its tributaries — Late May and early June.
Alexander Creek — Late May and early June.
Lower reaches of Lake Creek — Late May and early June.
Talachulitna River — May through September.
Coal Creek — May through September.
Upper reaches of Lake Creek — May through September.
Above waters are accessible by floatplane or riverboat only.
Big Susitna area (east side tributaries) — Same time as above.
Seventeen Mile, Harriet and Long Lakes (Matanuska Valley area) — Same as above.

KENAI PENINSULA

* Bait: Flies and small spinners.

Grayling Lake, Seward area — June through September.
Bench Lake, Moose Pass area — June through September.
Fuller and Crescent Lakes, near Cooper Landing — June through September.
Above lakes are accessible by trail.
Twin Lakes and Lower Paradise Lakes — June through September.
Above lakes are accessible by floatplane.

(Fish the outlets of all these lakes.)

ARCTIC GRAYLING (Continued)

KODIAK ISLAND

* Bait: Dry flies or spinners when shore fishing.

Cascade, Aurel, Abercrombie and Long Lakes ____ June through September.

BRISTOL BAY

* Bait: Flies and small spinners.

Ugashik Lake ____ July and August-peak.
Record-breaking grayling.

Grayling are abundant throughout the entire Bristol Bay region.

FAIRBANKS AND NORTHERN ALASKA

* Bait: Flies and small spinners.

The larger grayling can be caught in early spring and late fall in the headwaters of the streams listed below.

Tangle Lakes system ____ April 1st through September.
Delta Clearwater, Goodpaster, Salcha, Chena and Chatanika Rivers ____ April 1st through September.
These are all excellent grayling waters.
Sinuk, Niukluk and Fish Rivers (Nome area) ____ April 1st through September.
Lunker grayling are common in this region.
Unalakleet River, Norton Sound ____ April 1st through September.
Upper Yukon River, the tributary of Nation River (downstream from Eagle) ____ April 1st through September.

(Continued)

ARCTIC GRAYLING (continued)

COPPER RIVER-PRINCE WILLIAM SOUND

* Bait: Eggs are best when water is cloudy. Flies and small lures in clear water during fall months. Peaks in May and June, during break-up.

Gulkana River ______ Summer months.
Mae West, George, Junction, Gillespie, Dick, Kay, Tolsona, Arizona and Twin Lakes ______ Summer months.
Small roadside streams along the Glenn and Richardson Highways ______ Summer months.

SOUTHEASTERN ALASKA

* Bait: Small flies, shrimp and spinners.

Antler Lake, Juneau area ______ Early spring and late fall best.
Beaver Lake, Sitka area ______ Early spring and late fall best.
Big Goat, Manzoni and Snow Lakes, Ketchikan ______ Early spring and late fall best.

Grayling were first stocked in Southeastern in 1962 and there are current reports of catches weighing two pounds and over.

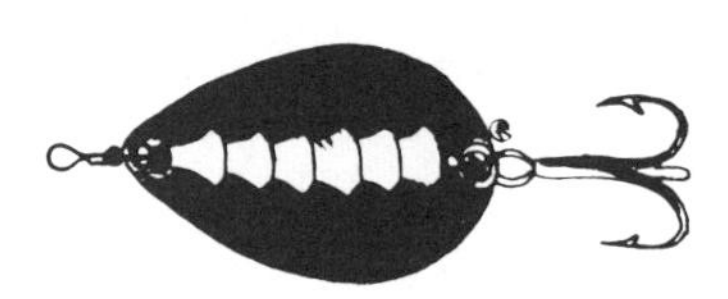

NORTHERN PIKE

(Also called pike or jackfish.)

RANGE AND DESCRIPTION

The northern pike's home waters in Alaska roughly parallel the range of the lake trout and burbot. It is found in the lakes, rivers, and sloughs of interior Alaska to the Arctic coast, from the Canadian border to the Seward Peninsula, and southwest to the Bristol Bay drainages.

An isolated population of pike is found in the Ahrnklin River, 10 miles southwest of Yakutat.

Like the burbot, the pike has an elongated head and body. The snout is broad and flat, somewhat like a duck bill. Hundreds of needle-sharp teeth line the roof of the mouth, jaws, tongue, and gill rakers. In color, the pike is extremely variable. A fish from a clear stream or lake will usually be light green, while pike taken from a dark slough or river will be much darker. The belly is light colored, whitish or yellow. The marking on the sides form irregular rows of yellow or gold spots. There is one soft-fin dorsal fin located far back on the body.

The females of this species live longer than the males, and they grow to a much larger size.

Spawning occurs soon after the ice goes out in early spring.

Overwinter areas of the jackfish are usually the deep, slow waters of larger rivers. Movement of the pike is usually minimal during summer months.

The major pike fishing areas are generally limited to access by airplane or riverboat. Some of the better locations are as follows: the Minto Flats area west of Fairbanks; clear water tributaries and sloughs of the Yukon and Kuskokwim Rivers; George, Healy, Mansfield and East and West Twin Lakes in interior Alaska. The Innoko River (in the Yukon drainage), Lake Minchumina, Kantishna River, Selawik Lake, and the Kobuk River all offer excellent pike fishing.

Trophy size fish are very common in the Tolovana and lower Chatanika Rivers, and in Goldstream Creek.

This species of fish has a voracious appetite and will strike at any bright moving lure. Spinners, spoons, plugs, and bucktail flies are all good.

Two necessary items that should be included in the pike fisherman's tackle box are wire leaders and a pair of long-nosed pliers.

The present Alaska State record pike is a 38-pound fish landed by a woman angler, Rhonda Edward at Fish Creek in 1978.

Trophy-size Northern pike, 15 pounds plus.

NORTHERN PIKE

FAIRBANKS AND NORTHERN AREA

* Bait: Plugs, spinners, spoons and bucktail flies. Bright colors are best.

Harding, Volkman, Mineral, George, Healy, Sand, Mansfield,
Wolf, Fish, Tetlin and Island Lakes ____ June through mid-September.

Moose, Chisana (near Tok) and Tolovana Rivers ____ June through mid-September.

Minto Flats area, west of Fairbanks ____ June through mid-September.

Provides the best pike fishing in the state. It is accessible by car, boat or floatplane.

Lower Tolovana, Chatanika and Tatalina Rivers,
Lower Goldstream Creek, and Minto Lakes ____ June through mid-September.

Trophy size pike are found in these waterways.

East Twin and Wien Lakes, (lunkers) ____ June through mid-September.

Yukon and Kuskokwim Rivers ____ Summer months.

The fresh water tributaries and sloughs of these rivers have large numbers of pike.

SHEEFISH

RANGE AND DESCRIPTION

This unique cold water fish is virtually unknown outside of Alaska. Its limited range is throughout the Kuskokwim, Kobuk, Selawik, and the Yukon River drainages.

During summer, the best sheefish fishing can be had along the Kobuk River in the Kiana, Ambler, and Kobuk areas, and also in Selawik Lake, Selawik River and the Tuklomarak River.

A local name for the sheefish is *inconnu*, meaning unknown fish. In Russia, it is called the *white salmon*, and nearer home, it has been described as the *shovel-nose whitefish*, the *shee*, or the *cony*.

It is a member of the whitefish family, and in shape is slender, with a long, tapering head. The scales of the sheefish are very large, and it is silver in color, light on the belly, darkening along the back.

This acrobatic fish grows to an impressive size — 60 pounds is not uncommon. The current Alaska State record is 52½ pounds. It was taken from the Kobuk River by Jim Keeline in 1968.

Shallow, brackish lakes such as Selawik Lake are home to many sheefish during a good part of the year.

Spawning runs start up the Kobuk, Selawik, and Tuklomarak Rivers after the ice break-up in June. The actual spawning does not occur until September, when the water temperature has dropped to 35 or 36 degrees.

Artifical lures are best to use. Daredevil spoons have proved to be most productive, with the hot rod and Nebco lures a close second.

The flesh of the sheefish is white, flaky and very tasty.

Trophy-size Sheefish, 30 pounds plus.

FAIRBANKS AND NORTHERN ALASKA

* Bait: Daredevil spoons.

Selawik Lake, Kotzebue Sound — Year round.
Hotham Inlet — Late spring for ice fishing.
Kobuk River (Kiana, Ambler and Kobuk areas) — Summer and fall.
Excellent fishing.
Selawik River and Tuklomarak River — Summer and fall.
Excellent fishing.
Holitna and Hoholitna Rivers, at Sleetmute — Summer and fall.
Koyukuk and Nowitna Rivers, tributaries to the Yukon River — Same as above.
Upper Chatanika River, near the Steese and Elliott Highways — Fall months.
Limited numbers of sheefish during fall months.
Fourmile Lake, on the Taylor Highway — Fall months.
Limited numbers of sheefish.
Tanana and Chena Rivers — Fall months.
These rivers produce a few sheefish; try the mouths of clearwater tributaries.

WHITEFISH

RANGE AND DESCRIPTION

Of the seven small species of whitefish in Alaska, the humpback is the most widely distributed. It ranges over the Interior and Northern Alaska, including the Chukchi and Bering Sea drainages, the Yukon and Kuskokwim River drainages, and Bristol Bay. The Copper, Susitna and Alsek River drainages are also good whitefish waters. This fish is native to a wide spectrum of habitats. It can be found in lakes, streams (both swift-flowing and slow-moving) and in clear mountain streams with gravel or sandy beds, or in brackish, tundra area water-ways.

The many variations of whitefish included in Alaskan waters are: the humpback, broad, least cisco, arctic cisco, Bering cisco, pygmy, and the round whitefish.

This sporty, cold-water fish normally feeds on larvae, water and land insects, and fish eggs. Broken down into specifics, the insects supplying the bulk of the white-fish diet are: mosquitoes, stone files, mayflies, true flies, and caddis. Midge larvae are the most important food to some species of the whitefish. Small worms bring good results in certain waters.

This northern fish has a small mouth, large scales, and is usually a silvery, or whitish color, with a darker back. The size varies with the locality. For example, whitefish landed from the Kobuk River average under two pounds, while those taken from the Chatanika River near Fairbanks can go over 21 inches in length.

Spear fishing for whitefish is allowed in the Tanana River drainage, particularly the upper Chatanika River. September and October are the best months, but remember to check with the local Alaska Department of Fish and Game for current regulations regarding spear fishing.

A seven-pound, two-ounce giant holds the current Alaska state record. It measured 25⅛ inches and was landed by Glen W. Cornwall from the Tolovana River in 1978.

FAIRBANKS AND NORTHERN ALASKA

* Bait: Small worms and flies.

Tanana River drainage ________ September and October.
Excellent spear fishing.

Upper Chatanika River ________ September and October.
Excellent spear fishing.

Delta Clearwater River, near Delta Junction ________ Spring and summer months.
Most Interior and Arctic Alaska streams and lakes contain whitefish. These fish are more difficult to catch than most Alaskan sportsfish. Regulations on spearfishing are subject to change. Check with the Department of Fish and Game.

BURBOT

(Also called fresh water ling, lush, or eelpout.)

RANGE AND DESCRIPTION

The burbot is the only fresh water member of the codfish family. Its appearance belies its excellent taste. To look at the ugly eel-like body, with its chin whisker and two dorsal fins (which run to the tail), and the dark, yellow mottled color, an uninitiated angler would never believe the gourmet table fare this fish can be.

Its habitat extends west to the Bering Sea, north to the Arctic Ocean, the Bristol Bay region and interior Alaskan waters (excluding the Upper Cook Inlet drainage and the Kenai Peninsula).

The Copper River supports the burbot in limited numbers.

The state record is currently the 24-pound, 12-ounce (three-feet. seven-inch) giant taken in Lake Lousie by George R. Howard in 1976.

This fish prefers the cold water of the deeper Alaskan lakes, although our northern waters produce burbot in many streams and lakes of all sizes.

The fresh-water ling does not mature sexually until it reaches an age of four to seven years and a length of 12 to 18 inches. Spawning occurs during February, March, and April.

Preferred angling for the burbot is through the ice during winter months, using set lines and baited single hooks. As mature burbot predominantly feed upon other fish, the best bait to use is the head or tail of a whitefish, lake trout, or smelt. Regulations and methods used are a little more complex for burbot fishing than for other sports fish, so it is best to refer to the State Fish and Game regulation hand book for current information.

Trophy-size Burbot, 8 pounds plus.

COPPER RIVER-PRINCE WILLIAM SOUND

* Bait: Pieces of herring or whitefish.

Ice fishing is best for burbot.

Louise, Susitna, Leila, Hudson, Crosswind, Paxson, and Summit Lakes.

FAIRBANKS AND NORTHERN ALASKA

* Bait: Pieces of herring or whitefish.

Chena and Tanana Rivers, near Fairbanks ______ Winter months.
Moose and Chisana Rivers, near Tok ______ Winter months.
George, Harding and Fielding Lakes ______ Winter months.

SALTWATER SECTION

Salmon Derbies

Salmon Fishing
Sea-run Dollies
Halibut
Rockfish
Bottomfish
Eulachon
Clams ● Crab

WHERE TO GO, AND HOW TO CATCH 'EM

SALMON FISHING DERBIES IN ALASKA

Because salmon derby rules and prize money offered are subject to change from season to season, the information offered here on derbies is not complete.

The author has listed the major derbies throughout the state, so the sports fisherman will know where the action is. If further information is needed on opening dates, etc., the angler should write to the Chamber of Commerce of the specific city in which he or she is interested

KENAI PENINSULA

Seward Silver Salmon Derby Begins the second Saturday in August. It lasts 8½ days, round the clock. $10,000 will be given for turning in the specially marked fish sponsored by the Seward Chamber of Commerce, and $5,000 for turning in the specially marked salmon sponsored by various merchants. The prize list is long, beginning with the largest silver caught during the derby and paying day money, first fish caught, etc.

Anchor River King Salmon Derby Usually held the last two weekends in May and the first two weekends in June.
Prizes are awarded for the largest salmon, and the first one caught each weekend. There is a special prize for the mystery fish.

VALDEZ

Valdez Silver Salmon Derby Held in Aug. every year

UPPER COOK INLET

Upper Cook Inlet Salmon Derby Usually held mid-June to July 1st. Write Chamber of Commerce, Wasilla, Alaska.

SOUTHEASTERN ALASKA

Ketchikan Two salmon derbies are offered. One runs continuously from mid-May through June. The other is held on successive weekends in late May and early June.

Ketchikan King Salmon Derby Runs in July.

SALMON FISHING DERBIES IN ALASKA (Continued)

Juneau. August Salmon Derby.

Sitka Salmon Derby - Held the latter part of May and first week in June.

Craig Salmon Derby Held annually on two weekends in late May and early June.

Thorne Bay Salmon Derby Held annually on two weekends in late May and early June. King salmon of 60 to 70 pounds usually win these derbies.

Juneau's Golden North Salmon Derby Held three day in August. Usually in the middle of the month. Prize money of $60,000 has been given in previous years.

Wrangell Salmon Derby From mid-May to early June.

Haines Salmon Derby Two derbies are run in Haines. One begins the end of May and extends through the first week in June. The other starts the 1st of June & continues for one week.

SALTWATER FISHING IN ALASKAN WATERS

A fishing license is necessary for saltwater fishing. When the license is purchased, be sure to pick up a current copy of *Alaska Sport Fishing Seasons and Bag Limits* booklet. This publication is put out by the Alaska Department of Fish and Game. Bag limits are subject to change, as are closures and some regulations.

General fishing hints are listed below.

Best times morning, early evening and during tide changes.

Kings - Generally caught at 40 to 90 foot depth at mid-day hours. Closer to the surface early mornings and evenings. May and June are peak seasons, 30 feet of water or less. Troll slowly with 22 to 37 feet of line out.

Silvers - Near the surface (the top 30 feet of water). Troll faster than for kings, with 15 to 30 feet of line out. The silvers prefer brighter colored lures, and chrome flashers or dodgers, with herring. Bait: herring for both kings and silvers. Fish where the current is moving (or near these spots). Tide rips, off beaches with high cliffs, or points jutting out from shore.

KING SALMON

SOUTHEASTERN ALASKA

* Bait: Trolled or drifted herring.

Bell Island at Ketchikan ________ Mid-March to September
Craig ________ Mid-March to September
Zimovia Straits, near Wrangell ________ Mid-March to September
Scow and Pybus Bays, near Petersburg ________ Mid-March to September
Saginaw Channel, near Tee Harbor, Juneau ________ Mid-March to September
Sitka Sound, near Sitka ________ Mid-March to September
Yakutat Bay, at Yakutat ________ Mid-March to September

Upper Lynn Canal and local inlets early summer months
Above waters, fishing peaks mid-May to mid-June.

KING SALMON (Continued)

KENAI PENINSULA

* Bait: Deep trolling with Golf 'Tee' spoons, other bright spoons, or herring.

Lunker kings can be caught throughout Cook Inlet waters. Peak months are May through July. Use number 5 and 6 spoons and herring.

Ninilchik River Kings to 60 pounds, fish in salt water off the mouth of the river mid-May through June.

Deep Creek Probably the most popular king salmon fishing spot on the Kenai Peninsual. Fish from one mile south of the mouth along the beachline, two-hundred yards at high tide, further if the tide is out. Late May, June, and July. Trolling a spoon or spinner is the preferred method.

Anchor Point Kings up to 50 pounds, June and July. Drift fish or troll an okie drifter or spin-n-glow, or herring.

Homer waters Kings are caught year round. Up until 1980, some of the better king fishing was in November and December. These were the months when the lunker *white* kings were caught. The season wasn't as productive in 1980. Troll with small herring and a *pink lady*. Sometimes a fluorescent bare spoon works well.

Kachemak Bay Kings up to 70 pounds. June and July are peak seasons.

Seldovia Bay King salmon fishing good. June 20th through September, use large spinners.

KODIAK ISLAND

Karluk River Excellent king salmon fishing off the mouth, beginning in early June and continuing through the month.

COPPER RIVER-PRINCE WILLIAM SOUND

* Bait: Herring or large trolling lures are preferred.

Late winter and early spring.

SILVER SALMON

KENAI PENINSULA

* Bait: Herring or small spoons or spinners. (Trolling or mooching.)

Resurrection Bay at Seward —— Early July, peaking in mid-August and ending in early September. (Occasionally extending to late September.)

Kachemak Bay, near Homer —— August.

Cook Inlet —— Late July through August. (Between Cape Ninilchik and Anchor Point along the beach line.)

The silver prefers a rapidly moving, erratic lure. It is a surface feeder, as opposed to a bottom feeder, as the king salmon usually is.

SEA—RUN CUTTHROAT AND DOLLY VARDEN

SOUTHEASTERN ALASKA

* Bait: Eggs, flies, and spoons are all good.

Fish the vicinity of river and stream mouths —— May to October.

SEA—RUN DOLLY VARDEN

KENAI PENINSULA

* Bait: Same as above.

Kachemak Bay —— Early spring through fall. Peaks in July and August. Most southside beaches and stream mouths are good.

Homer Spit —— Early spring through fall. Peaks in July and August. Shore angling can bring results.

SEA-RUN DOLLY VARDEN (Continued)

KODIAK

* Bait: Herring strips work well, also small and medium-sized lures.

Most of the rocky beaches ———————————————— June through July.

COPPER RIVER-PRINCE WILLIAM SOUND

* Bait: Salmon eggs, flies and a wide variety of spinners and lures are productive.

Fish the vicinity of river and creek mouths ———————————— During salmon runs in the fall.

HALIBUT

The Pacific halibut ranges in size up to 400 pounds. Anglers in Alaskan waters often catch fish in the 100 to 200 pound class. The current state record is a 440 pounder, taken at Point Adolphus in 1978 by Joar Savland.

Good halibut fishing can be had in many regions of the state: Southeastern, Kenai Peninsula, Kodiak Island, and Prince William Sound.

Fish the small bays and inlets in Prince William Sound, jigging with large lures and bait. In the Kodiak offshore area, especially off Long and Woody Island, summer months are more productive as the fish become more active.

Late August is the peak halibut season in Southeastern inland waters, although these fish may be caught from May to September here. Octopus and herring are preferred baits, and jigging with large spoons is also productive.

In the Kenai Peninsula region, the top halibut waters are from Deep Creek area south to Kachemak Bay. Kachemak Bay and the Cook Inlet area is probably one of the top halibut fishing spots of the world. There is a good selection of halibut charter boats based on Homer Spit.

In all regions try razor clams or herring, worked over a sandy bottom, or jig with bait or large silver colored lures. Halibut are bottom feeders, best fished in waters of from 20 to 40 fathoms deep.

Wire leaders are essential to use. (18 inch minimum.) The line should be 50 to 80 pound test. Hook size should be from 9/0 to 12/0. A gaff hook is necessary, as is a heavy boat rod of from 6 foot to 8 foot, and a star-drag reel.

If the angler is after sport; not a meat fisherman, try sports tackle. It is more of a challenge to play and boat a halibut using salmon gear.

Trophy-size halibut, 100 pounds plus.

HALIBUT (Continued)

KENAI PENINSULA

* Bait: Herring or any oily fish. Try jigging with a large spoon ———— trolling will bring results.

Lower Cook Inlet from the Deep Creek area south to Kachemak Bay.

KODIAK ISLAND

* Bait: Same as above.

Long and Woody Islands contain the heaviest concentration of halibut, although these fish are plentiful in the entire offshore area. The season is year-round, although summer months are best.

COPPER RIVER-PRINCE WILLIAM SOUND

* Bait: Same as above.

Halibut are plentiful in most of Prince William Sound. They will be found in more concentrated numbers in the small bays of the Sound.

SOUTHEASTERN ALASKA

* Bait: Same as above, with the addition of octopus.

Common throughout the entire region ———— May to September, peaking in August in inside waters.

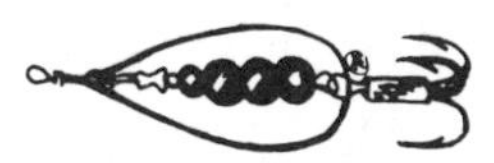

ROCKFISH (Includes the red snapper, and the black rockfish.)

KENAI PENINSULA

Resurrection Bay--in the vicinity of Cheval and Rugged Islands.

KODIAK ISLAND

Shallow waters near kelp beds, or by rocky outcroppings.

SOUTHEASTERN ALASKA

600 feet is not too deep to find these bottom feeders.

Fish near rocky areas.

* Bait: Any fish or meat, and bright lures.

BOTTOMFISH (Includes the Pacific cod and tomcod, the whiting or walley pollock, sole, flounder, sable fish, Irish Lord, ling cod, and greenling.)

Along with the halibut and rockfish already mentioned, the rich waters and rocky bays of Southeastern, Prince William Sound, Kenai Peninsula, and Kodiak Island all afford good bottomfish angling.

EULACHON **(A form of smelt, this fish is also called hooligan, or candlefish.)**

When the spring hooligan run is on, most of the fishing population of Upper and Lower Cook Inlet rustle up hip waders and fine mesh dip nets, and head for the spawning streams.

Placer and Twentymile rivers are the waterways near Portage used for spawning by the eulachon. In the Seward area, it is the mouth of Resurrection River. This oily fish is nick-named *candlefish* because of its fat content. When the fish have been dried and a wick drawn through them, they can be burned like a candle.

The size of the mature fish at the time of the spawning run varies from eight to 14 inches. May and June is the season for Lower Cook Inlet migrations. Southeastern Alaska eulachon runs occur during May in the Chilkat River near Haines.

Bristol Bay has its hooligan migration also. This does not begin until early June, when the estuary areas of the Nushagak become invaded by hordes of silver smelt.

Check current regulations with the Department of Fish and Game, as the bag limit for eulachon is not per fish, but per pound.

UPPER COOK INLET

These small fish are taken by dip net during the spawning run in May.

Placer and Twentymile Rivers, near Portage.

KENAI PENINSULA

Resurrection River, near Seward.

Lower Kenai ———— Late May.

A special subsistence gill net fishery occurs in late May. Contact the Department of Fish and Game for information on regulations.

CLAMS

Spring and summer months--minus tides.

KENAI PENINSULA

Razor clams are found on most of the sandy beaches of the western Kenai Peninsula, from Kasilof to Anchor Point.

Clam Gulch Accessible via the Sterling Highway, it is the most productive and easily reached of the clamming beaches on the Peninsula.

Happy Valley Creek Mile 195.6 —— south of Anchorage, good clamming on the sandy beaches at the mouth of this creek. A sports fishing license is required to dig clams and can be purchased at most sporting goods stores. Bag limit is 60 clams, regardless of size, open season is year round. Clams are of a better quality beginning in April and extending through August.

NOTE: A Fish and Game booklet is published on razor clams in the Cook Inlet area. It contains information on where and how to dig, and the regulations currently in effect. These are available at most local offices of the State Fish and Game Department.

RAZOR CLAMS

COOK INLET AREA

Along the east side of the Inlet.

The most accessible beaches are those from Kasilof River to Anchor Point.

The top clamming beach in this area is Clam Gulch, located 22 miles south of Soldotna.

Along the west side of the Inlet.

Clam beach at Polly Creek.

South of Cape Douglas is Swickshak clam beach, on Shelikof Strait.

CORDOVA AREA AND SOUTH ALONG THE ALASKA PENINSULA

Good clam beaches.

*Note--Recommended minimum of minus 3.0 foot tides for Deep Creek and Happy Valley on the Kenai Peninsula.

LITTLENECK CLAMS

This type of clam is available in most gravel-mud beaches in protected bays at half-tide level in Valdez Arm and Prince William Sound.

(Continued)

COCKLES

Cockle clams are found on the east side of the Homer Spit, on the Kenai Peninsula.

HARDSHELL CLAMS

These can be taken along the southern beaches of Kachemak Bay. McDonald Spit is the most popular site in this area.

NOTE: A free booklet on Cook Inlet razor clam digging is available at most offices of the Department of Fish and Game.

CRAB

(King, Dungeness and Tanner are native to Alaskan waters.)

The King Crab is the largest of the Alaskan crab. Its habitat ranges from Southeastern Alaska to the Bering Sea. An average male would weigh from six to seven pounds, but weights of over 20 pounds are not uncommon. Crab pots for the King crab must be set in deep water of 30 to 50 fathoms. The bait used is normally herring, but any type of oily fish will do.

Size is the most obvious difference between the Dungeness and the king. The Dungeness will average two to three pounds. It is by far the easiest for the sportsman to take. The depths of water the smaller crab is found in is much shallower. Although the Dungeness can be found in deeper water, usually the best locations are the shallow saltwater lagoons and the shallows at the leads of bays.

The Tanner crab is the smaller of the three species. It has a spidery appearance, with legs that are very long and thin. This is a deep-water crab, usually found in the same habitat as the King.

KENAI PENINSULA

Kachemak Bay King to 12 pounds, Dungeness and Tanner crab can be caught during early spring months and late fall. Crab pots for king crab over three or four pounds. Sometimes bottom fishing with sports tackle, using herring for bait, will land one of the three available species of crab.

MAP SECTION

FISH SPECIES ABBREVIATIONS USED IN THIS SECTION

Arctic Char .... AC
Arctic Grayling .... GR
Burbot .... BB
Chum Salmon .... CS
Cutthroat Trout .... CT
Dolly Varden .... DV
Brook Trout .... BT
Halibut .... H
King Salmon .... KS
Lake Trout .... LT
Ling Cod LC
Northern Pike .... NP
Rainbow Trout .... RT
Red Salmon .... RS
Rockfish .... RF
Sheefish .... SF
Silver Salmon .... SS
Steelhead Trout .... SH
Whitefish .... WF

* For more detailed information on accessibility, types of fish in specific waters, etc., check with a Fish and Game office for booklet, "Alaska Sport Fishing Guide".

TABLE OF CONTENTS - -MAPS

MAP NO.	AREAS COVERED	PAGE
1	Alaska Highway (Boundary to Delta Junction)	74
2	Taylor Highway (40-Mile to Eagle)	75
3	Richardson Highway (Delta Junction to Fairbanks)	76
4	Parks Highway	77
5	Steese Highway	78
6	Elliott Highway	79
7	Brooks Range(Bettles Area)	80
8	Kotzebue-Kobuk, Fly-In Waters	83
9	Nome-Solomon-Teller Roads	84
10	Slana-Tok Cut-Off Highway	86
11	Richardson Highway (Valdez to Black Rapids)	88
12	Denali Highway	90
13	Glenn Highway	92
14	Palmer Highway and Matanuska Valley Roads	94
15	Willow-Talkeetna Area (Willow-Hatcher Pass Road)	96
15A	Parks Highway (Talkeetna to Summit)	98
16	Anchorage Area	99
17	Seward Highway (Anchorage to Seward)	100
18	Sterling Highway (Seward Highway Junction to Soldotna)	102
19	Skilak Loop Road	104
20	Sterling Highway (Kenai-Soldotna Area to Homer)	106
21	Bristol Bay-Alaska Peninsula Area	108
22	Kodiak Island	112
23	Afognak Island	114
24	Copper River Highway (Cordova)	115
25	Chitina-McCarthy Road	116
26	Yakutat Area	117
27	Haines and Skagway Area	118
28	Juneau Area	120
29	Admiralty Island	122
30	Sitka Area	124
31	Petersburg Area	126
32	Wrangell Area	127
33	Ketchikan Area	128

TIME OF ABUNDANCE CHART

Fish Species	*Abrev. Used*	*Best Bait or Lure*	*Max. Size*	*Time of Abundance*				
				Southeast	*Southcentral*	*Westward*	*Interior*	*Kodiak*
Arctic Char	AC	Spoon, Eggs	20 lbs.	Absent	June-Aug.	June-Sept.	July-Sept.	Absent
Arctic Grayling	GR	Flies	5 lbs.	July-Sept.	May-Sept.	May-Sept.	May-Oct.	Absent
Burbot	BB	Bait	30 lbs.	Absent	All Year	All Year	All Year	Absent
Chum Salmon	CS	Spoon	15 lbs.	July-Sept.	July-Aug.	July-Aug.	July-Sept.	July
Cutthroat Trout	CT	Bait, Spin., Flies	7 lbs.	May-Sept.	June-Sept.	Absent	Absent	Absent
Dolly Varden	DV	Bait, Spin., Flies	15 lbs.	May-Oct.	All Year	All Year	Absent	May-Oct.
Brook Trout	BT	Eggs, Spin.	5 lbs.	May-Sept.	Absent	Absent	Absent	Absent
Halibut	H	Octopus, Herring	300 lbs.	May-Oct.	All Year	All Year	Absent	May-Sept.
King Salmon	KS	Herring, Spoon	100 lbs.	April-July	May-July	May-Aug.	July-Aug.	June-July
Kokanee	Kok	Spin., Eggs	2 lbs.	May-Sept.	All Year	All Year	Absent	Absent
Lake Trout	LT	Spoon, Plug	45 lbs.	Absent	All Year	All Year	All Year	Absent
Ling Cod	LC	Herring	80 lbs.	All Year	All Year	All Year	Absent	All Year
Northern Pike	NP	Spoon, Spin.	30 lbs.	Absent	All Year	All Year	All Year	Absent
Pink Salmon	PS	Sm. Spoon	10 lbs.	July-Aug.	July-Aug.	July-Aug.	Absent	July-Aug.
Rainbow Trout	RT	Flies, Lures, Bait	20 lbs.	May-Sept.	All Year	All Year	All Year	All Year
Red Salmon	RS	Spoon, Flies	15 lbs.	June	June-July	June-Aug.	Absent	June-July
Rockfish	RF	Herring, Spin.	20 lbs.	All Year	All Year	All Year	Absent	All Year
Sheefish	SF	Spoon	50 lbs.	Absent	Absent	May-Sept.	July-Oct.	Absent
Silver Salmon	SS	Herring, Spoon	25 lbs.	July-Oct.	July-Sept.	July-Sept.	All Year	Sept.-Nov.
							landlocked	
Steelhead Trout	SH	Spoon, Eggs	45 lbs.	April-June	May-June	May-June	Absent	April-May
				Oct.-May	Aug.-Oct.	Aug.-Oct.		Sept.-Nov.
Whitefish	WF	Flies, Eggs	10 lbs.	All Yr. Haines	All Year	All Year	All Year	Absent

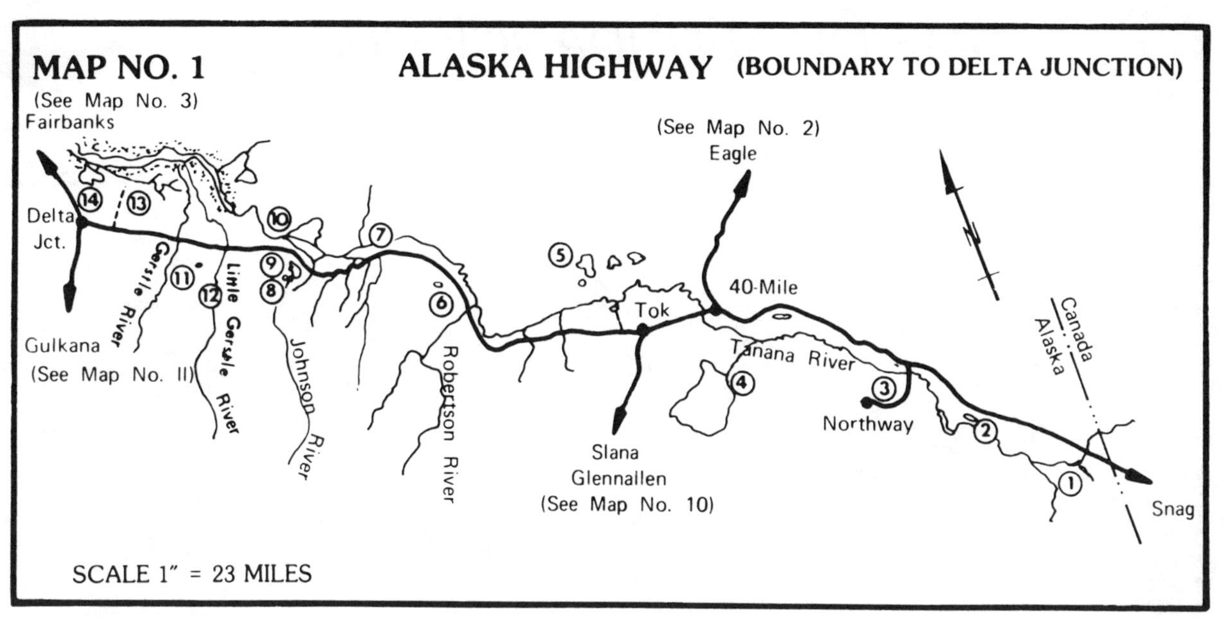

KEY NO.	WATERWAY	FISH SPECIES
1	Scottie Creek	GA, BB
2	Deadman Lake	NP, BB
3	Moose Slough	NP, BB
4	Tetlin Lake	NP, GR, WF, BB
5	Mansfield Lake	NP, BB
6	Jan Lake	SS, RT
7	Berry Creek	GR, BB
8	Lisa Lake	RT, SS
9	Craig Lakes	RT, SS
10	George Lake	NP, WF, BB
11	Donna Lake	RT, SS
12	Little Donna Lake	RT
13	Delta Clearwater River	GR, SS, WF, BB
14	Delta Clearwater Lake	GR, NP, WF, BB

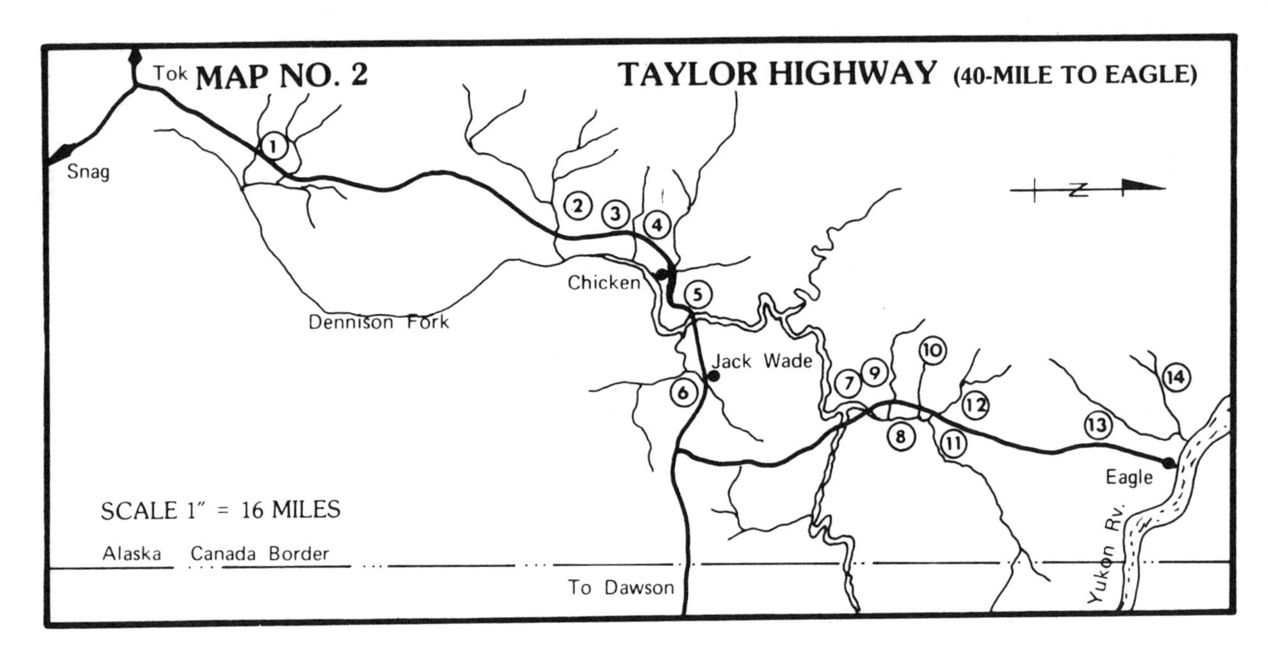

KEY NO.	WATERWAY	FISH SPECIES
1	Logging Cabin Creek	GR
2	West Fork of the Dennison	GR
3	Taylor Creek	GR
4	Mosquito Fork	GR
5	40-Mile River	GR, SF
6	Walker's Fork	GR
7	40-Mile River	GR, SF
8	O'Brien Creek	GR
9	Alder Creek	GR
10	Columbia Creek	GR
11	King Solomon Creek and Liberty Fork	GR
12	North Fork of King Solomon Creek	GR
13	American Creek	GR
14	Mission Creek	GR

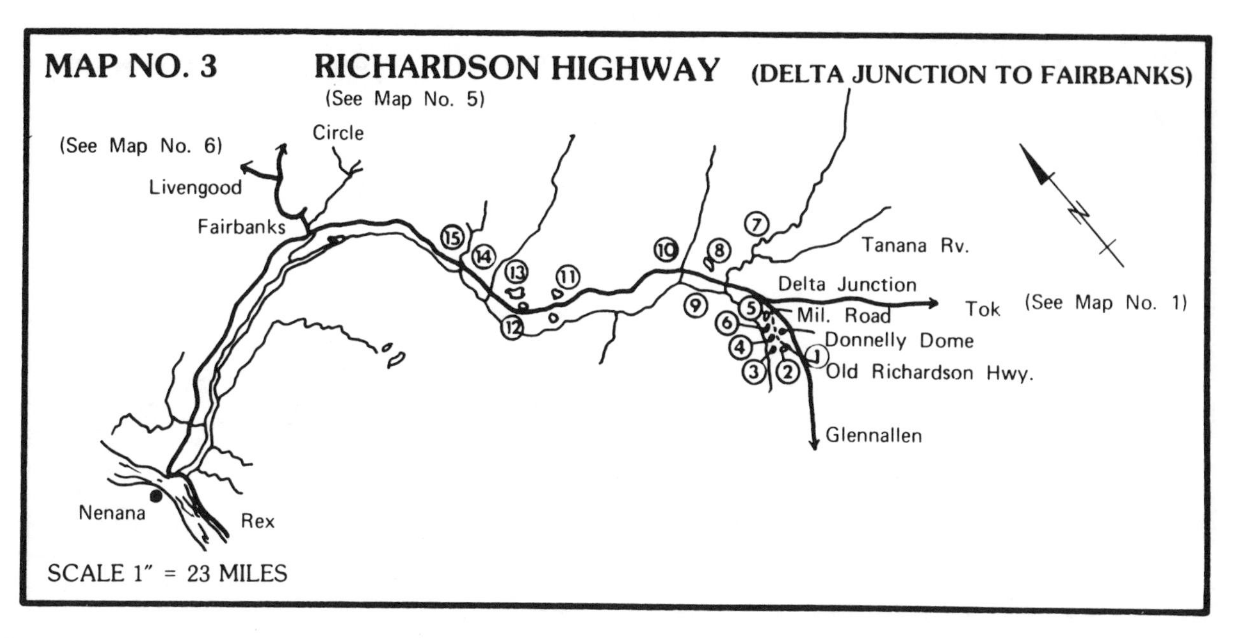

KEY NO.	WATERWAY	FISH SPECIES
1	Donnally Lake	SS
2	Nickel Lake	GR
3	Chet Lake	GR
4	"J" Lake	GR
5	Bolio Lake	SS
6	Mark Lake	RT
7	Goodpaster River	GR, WF
8	Quartz Lake	RT
9	81-Mile Lake	GR
10	Shaw Creek	GR, WF
11	Birch Lake	RT, SS
12	Harding Lake	NP, LT, BB, SS
13	Little Harding Lake	SS
14	Salcha River	GR, KS, CS
15	Little Salcha River	GR

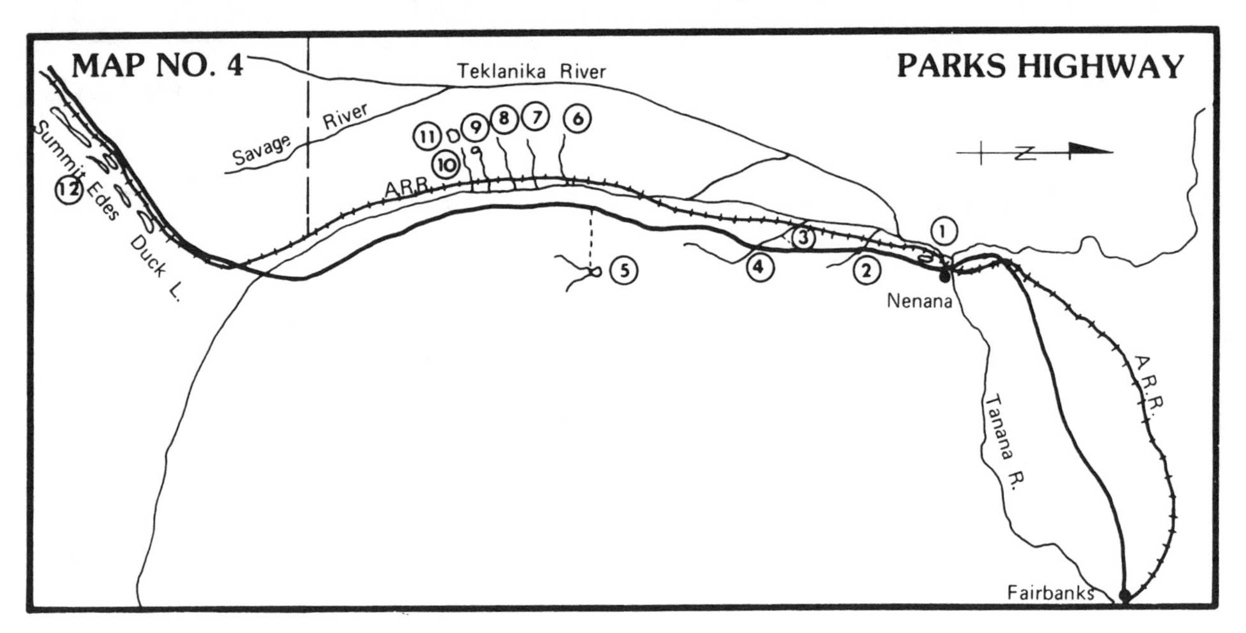

KEY NO.	WATERWAY	FISH SPECIES
1	Nenana Pond	GR
2	Fish Creek	GR
3	Julius Creek	GR
4	Julius Creek	GR
		NP, WF
6	Birch Creek	GR
7	Bear Creek	GR
8	Rock Creek	GR
9	Slate Creek	GR
10	Panguinge Creek	GR
11	Eight-Mile Lake	GR
12	Broad Pass Lakes	GR, WF, LT, BB

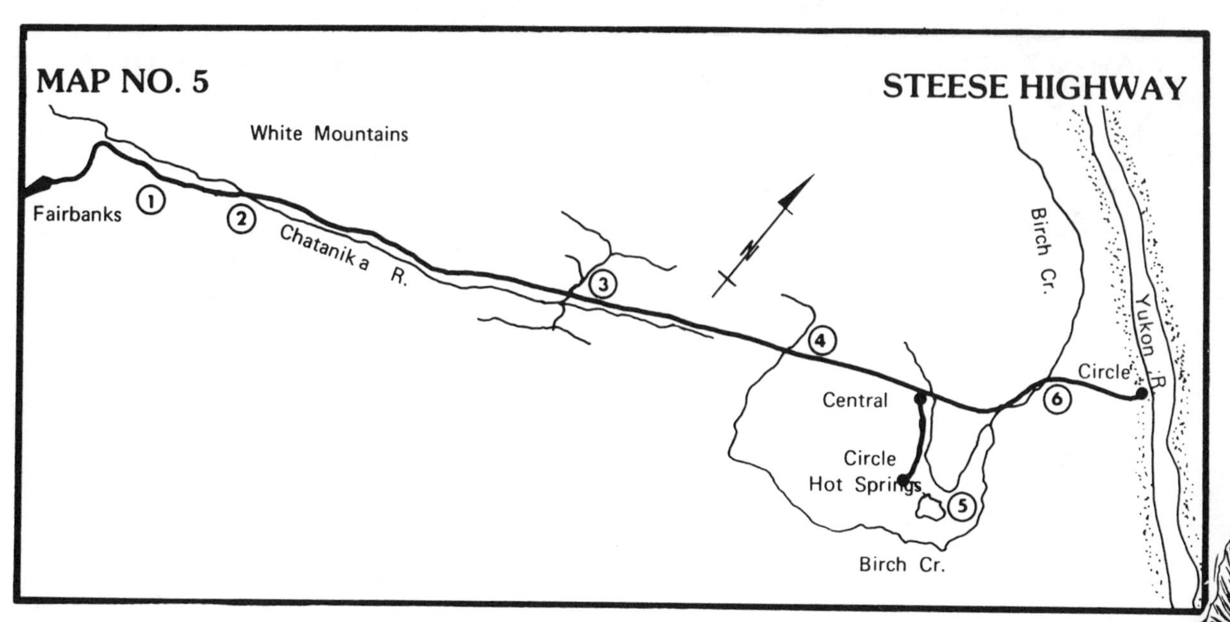

KEY NO.	WATERWAY	FISH SPECIES
1	Chatanika River	GR, NP, SF, KS, CS, SS, BB
2	Chatanika River	GR, NP
3	Faith Creek	GR, NP
4	North Fork of Birch Creek	GR, NP
5	Medicine Lake	NP, WF
6	Birch Creek	GR, NP

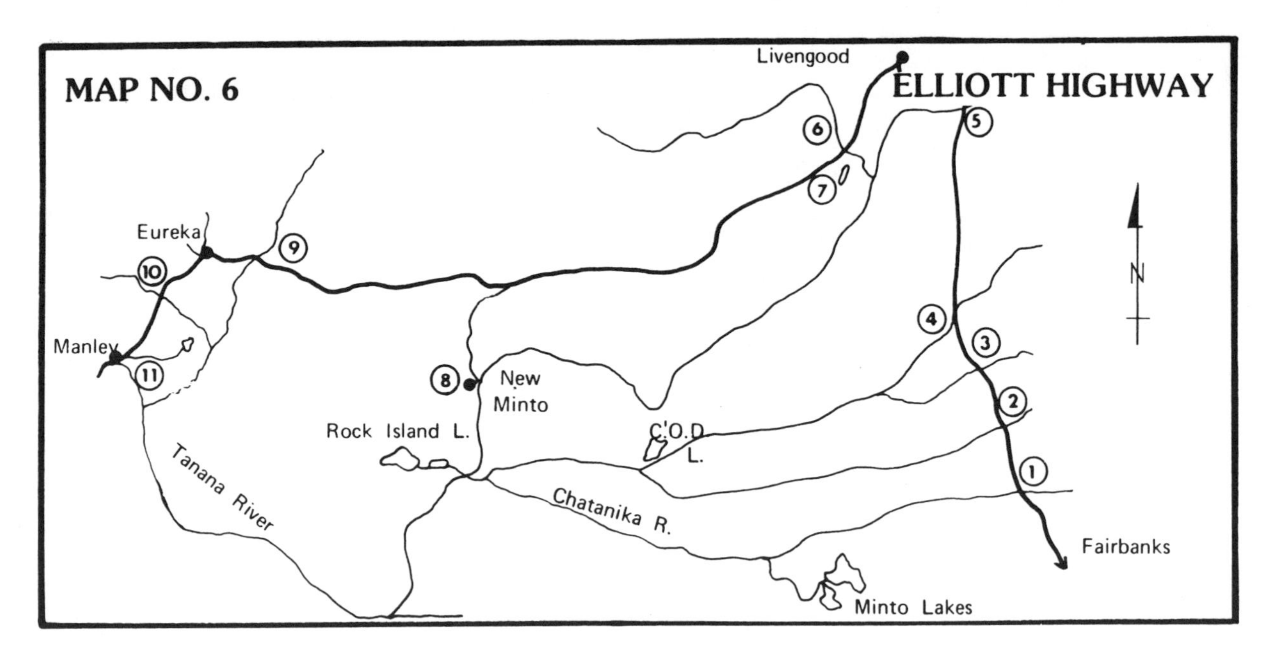

KEY NO.	WATERWAY	FISH SPECIES
1	Chatanika River	GR, WF, NP, KS
2	Washington Creek	GR
3	Globe Creek	GR
4	Tatalina River	GR, WF
5	Tolovana River	GR, WF
6	West Fork of the Tolovana River	GR, WF
7	Kuck Lake	NP
8	Minto Flats	NP, SF, WF, BB
9	Hutlinana Creek	GR, DV
10	Baker Creek	GR
11	Hot Springs Slough	NP, WF, SF

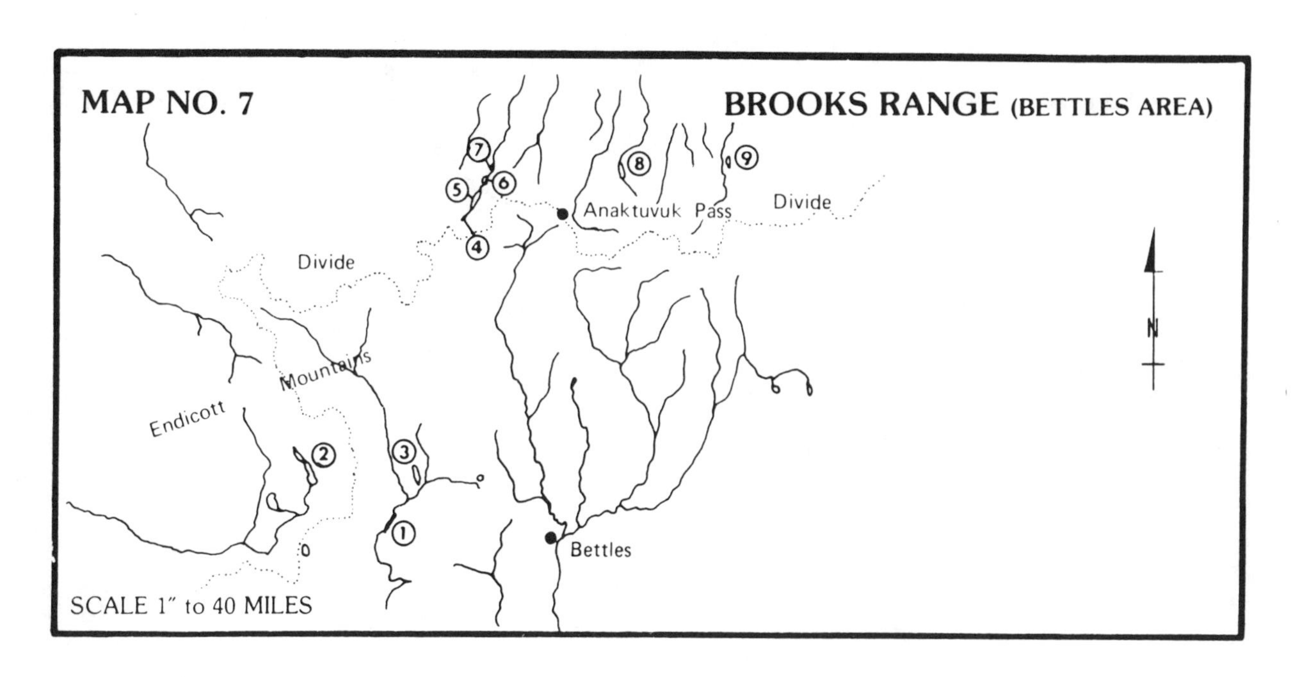

KEY NO.	WATERWAY	FISH SPECIES
1	Helpmejack Lake	LT, NP, WF
2	Walker Lake	LT, NP, WF, AC
3	Iniakuk Lake	LT, NP, WF
4	Fish Lake	LT, AC, GR, WF
5	Chandler Lake	LT, AC, GR, WF
6	Lower Chandler Lake	LT, AC, GR, WF
7	Round Lake	LT, AC, GR, WF
8	Shainin Lake	LT, AC, GR, WF
9	Nanuskuk Lake	LT, GR, WF

ARCTIC FISHING EXPEDITIONS
3 DAY TALKEETNA RIVER TRIP
LONGEST WHITE WATER STRETCH OF
ANY RIVER IN NORTH AMERICA
Trips designed for
Ultimate Arctic Fishing
Experience from 10 to 21 days
All inclusive from Anchorage
Kobuk River * Noatak River
Colville River * Chandalar River
Yukon River
nova
riverunners of alaska
SRC BOX 8337
PALMER, ALASKA, 99645
(907) 745-5753
Custom Trips upon
request

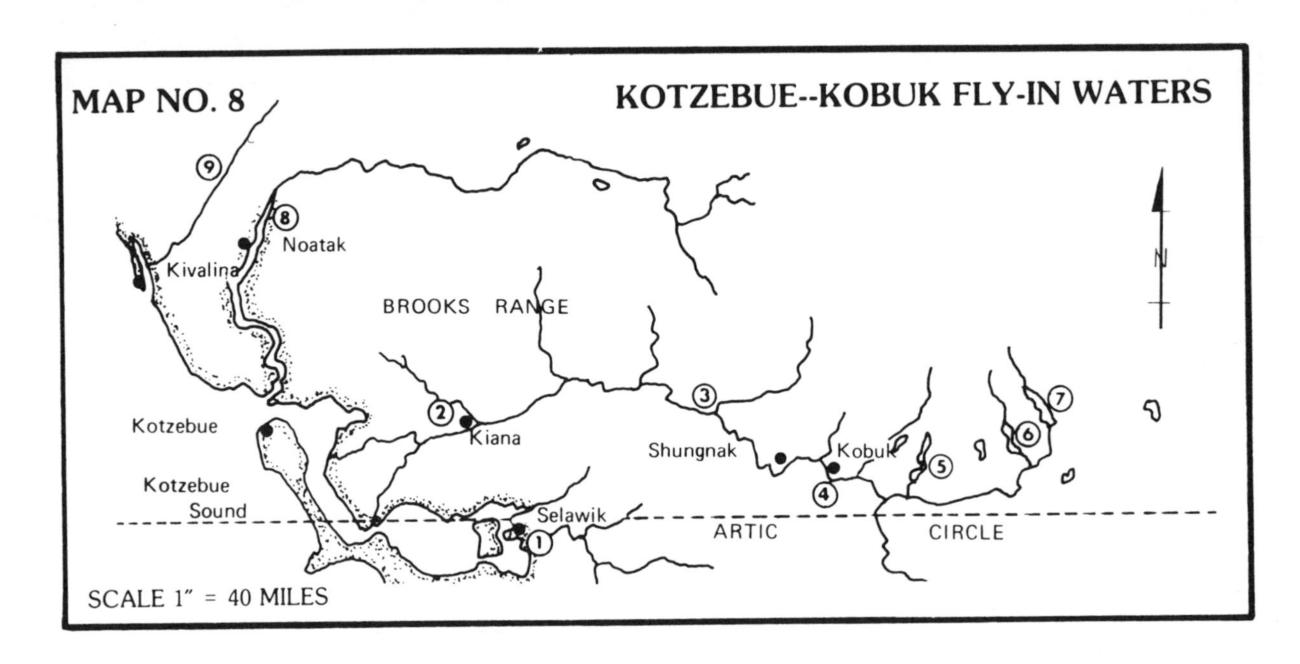

KEY NO.	WATERWAYS	FISH SPECIES
1	Selawik River	SF, NP
2	Kiana Village	SF
3	Kobuk River (lower)	SF, NP, GR
4	Kobuk River (upper)	SF, NP, GR, WF
5	Selby Lake	LT, GR, NP, BB
6	Nutuvukti Lake	LT, GR, NP, BB
7	Walker Lake	LT, GR, NP, BB, AC
8	Noatak River	AC, GR, CS
9	Wulik River	AC, GR

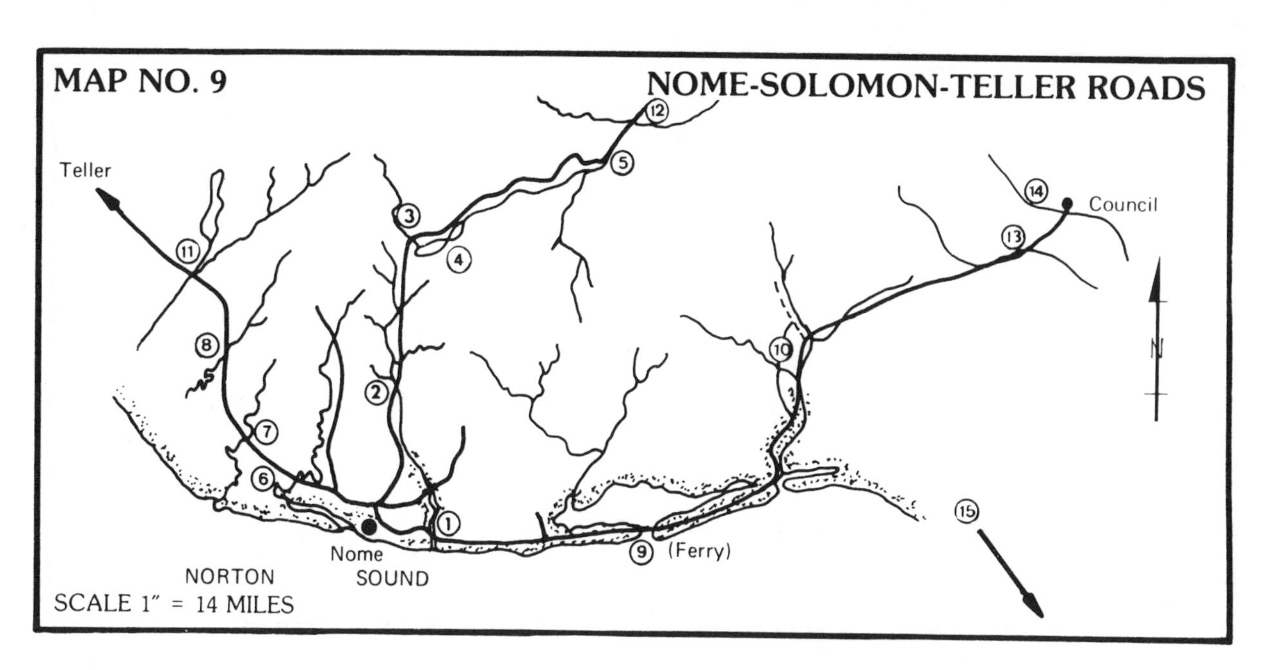
MAP NO. 9
NOME-SOLOMON-TELLER ROADS
Teller
Council
(Ferry)
Nome
NORTON
SOUND
N
SCALE 1" = 14 MILES

MAP NO. 9 NOME-SOLOMON-TELLER ROADS

KEY NO.	WATERWAYS	FISH SPECIES
1	Nome River	PS, DV, SS, CS, KS, AC, Flounder, Black Cod
2	Nome River	PS, DV, CS, KS, SS, GR, AC
3	Grand Central	GR, DV, WF, RS
4	Salmon Lake	RS, DV, CS, WF, GR,, NP
5	Pilgrim (Kruagamepa) River	PS, CS, SS, DV, WF, AC, NP
6	Snake River	CS, PS, SS, GR, DV, AC
7	Penny River	GR, AC
8	Cripple Creek	GR, AC
9	Safety Lagoon	PS, CS, AC, H, Flounder
10	Solomon River	PS, CS, GR, AC
11	Sinuk River	CS, PS, AC, DV, GR
12	Kuzitrin River	KS, CS, PS, AC, DV, GR, NP
13	Fox River	CS, PS, GR
14	Niuluk River	CS, PS, GR, WF, DV, AC, SS
15	Unalakleet River	KS, SS, PS, CS, DV, GR, AC

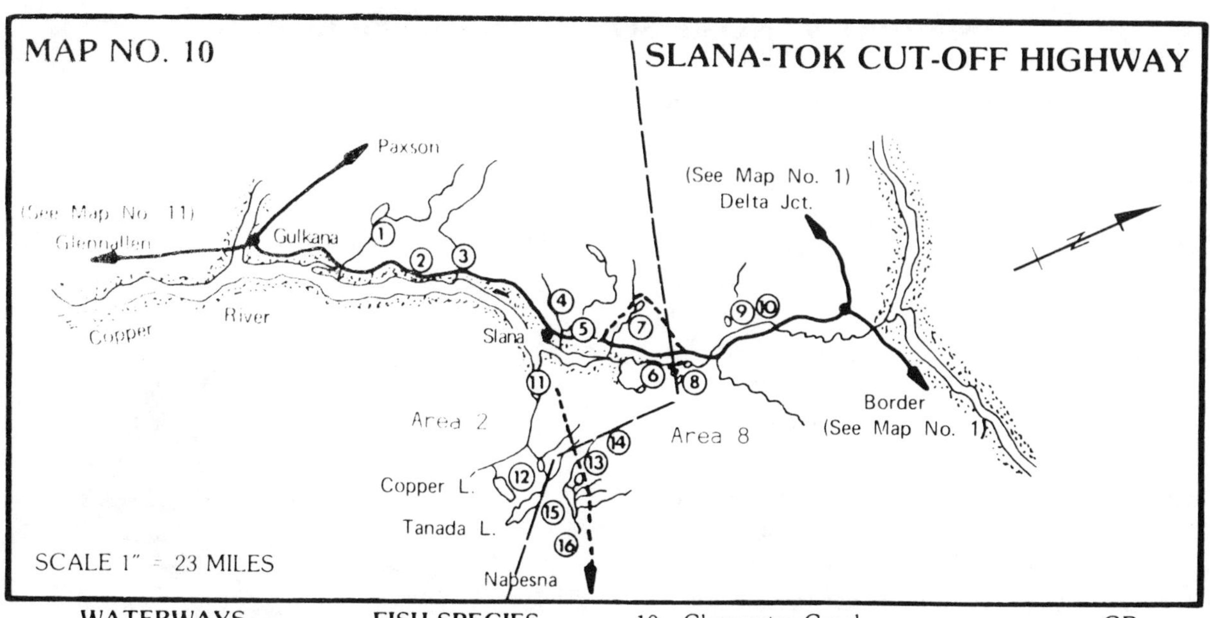

KEY NO.	WATERWAYS	FISH SPECIES
1	Tulsona Creek	GR
2	Gravel Pit Lake	GR
3	Sinona Creek	GR, DV
4	Ahtell Creek	GR
5	Carlson Creek	GR, DV
6	Mable Creek	GR
7	Mentasta Lake	GR, WF
8	Mineral Lake	GR, NP, WF
9	Tok Overflow #2	GR
10	Clearwater Creek	GR

NABESNA ROAD (MILE 60-SLANA TOK HIGHWAY)

KEY NO.	WATERWAYS	FISH SPECIES
11	Rufus Creek	DV
12	Long Lake	GR, BB
13	Little Twin Lake	GR, LT, BB
14	Big Twin Lake	GR, BB
15	Jack Lake	GR, WF, LT, BB
16	Jack Creek	GR

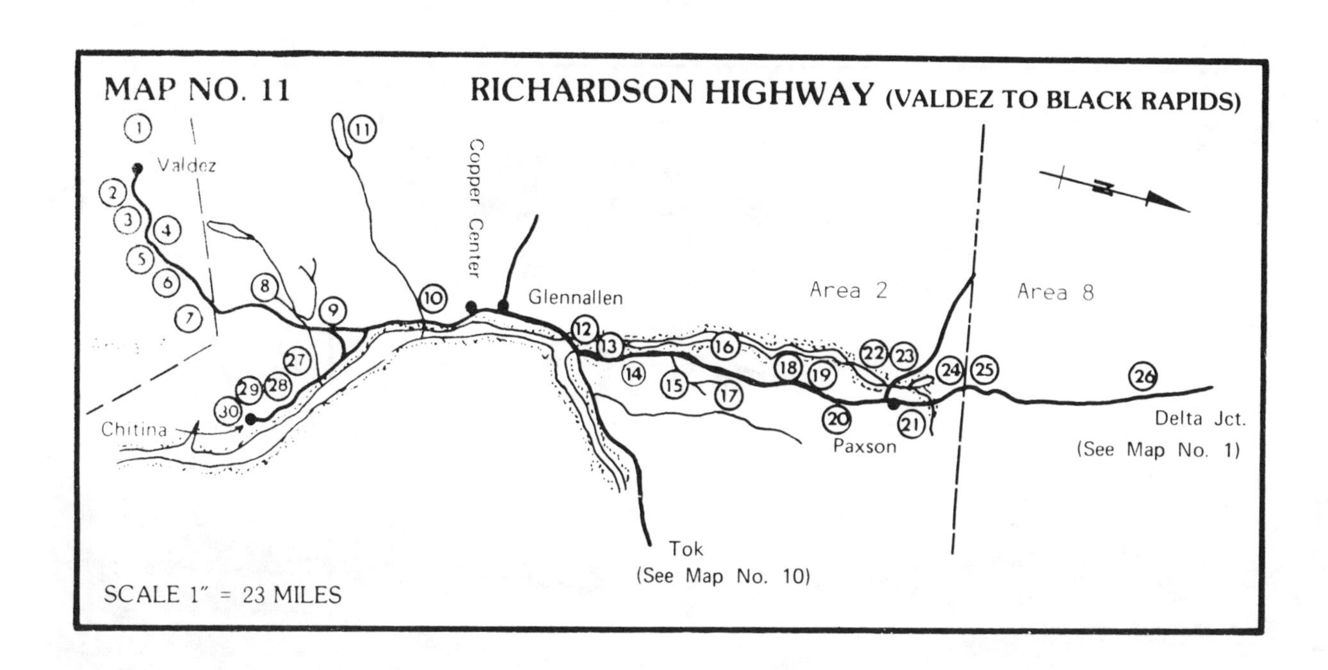
MAP NO. 11
RICHARDSON HIGHWAY (VALDEZ TO BLACK RAPIDS)
Valdez
Copper Center
Glennallen
Area 2
Area 8
Chitina
Paxson
Delta Jct.
(See Map No. 1)
Tok
(See Map No. 10)
SCALE 1" = 23 MILES
1
2
3
4
5
6
7
8
9
10
11
12
13
14
15
16
17
18
19
20
21
22
23
24
25
26
27
28
29
30

MAP NO. 11 RICHARDSON HIGHWAY (Valdez to Black Rapids)

KEY NO.	WATERWAYS	FISH SPECIES
1	Port Valdez	SS, KS, PS, CS, DV, Bottomfish
2	Robe River & Lake	DV
3	Lowe River	DV
4	Blueberry Lake	RT
5	Thompson Lake	GR
6	Worthington Lake	RT
7	Tiekel River	DV
8	Little Tonsina River	DV, GR
9	Squirrel River	GR
10	Klutina River	DV, GR, KS, RS
11	Klutina Lake	BB, DV, GR, LT, KS, RS
12	Bear Lake	GR
13	Gulkana River	RT, GR, KS, RS, WF
14	Poplar Grove	GR, WF
15	Sourdough Creek	GR
16	June and Nita Lakes	WF, GR
17	Haggard Creek	GR
18	Gillespie Lake & Creek	GR
19	Meirs Lake	GR
20	Dick Lake	GR
21	Paxson Lake	LT, GR, WF, BB
22	Mud Lake	GR
23	Fish Creek & Lakes	GR
24	Summit Lake	LT, GR, WF, BB
25	Fielding Lake	LT, GR, WF, BB
26	Rapid Lake	RT

EDGERTON CUT-OFF

KEY NO.	WATERWAYS	FISH SPECIES
27	Liberty Falls Creek	GR
28	3-Mile Lake	RT, GR
29	2-Mile Lake	RT, GR
30	Chitina (Town) Lake	GR, DV

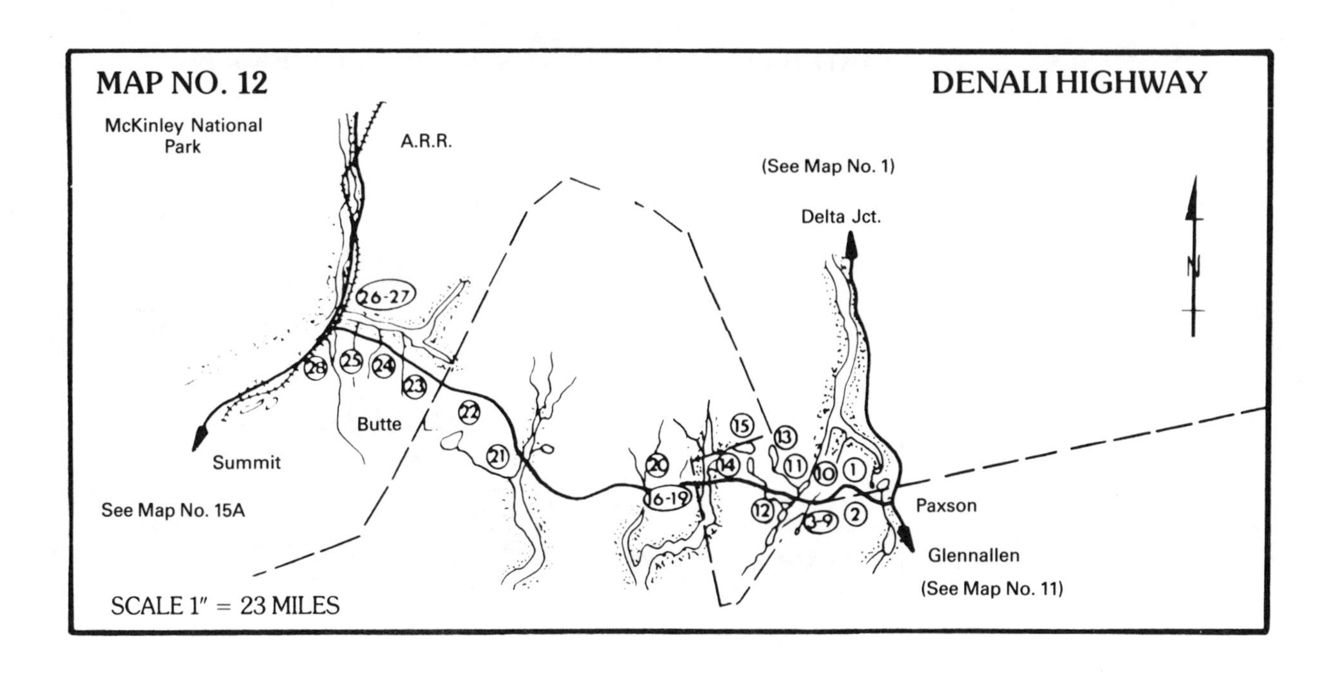
MAP NO. 12
DENALI HIGHWAY
McKinley National Park
A.R.R.
(See Map No. 1)
Delta Jct.
N
26-27
28
25
24
23
22
21
20
16-19
15
14
13
12
11
10
1
2
3-9
Butte L.
Summit
See Map No. 15A
Paxson
Glennallen
(See Map No. 11)
SCALE 1″ = 23 MILES

MAP NO. 12 DENALI HIGHWAY

KEY NO.	WATERWAY	FISH SPECIES
1	Seven-Mile L.	LT
2	Ten-Mile L.	LT,GR,WF,BB
3	Teardrop L.	LT,GR,BB
5	Octopus L.	LT,GR,WF,
5	Little Swede L.	LT
6	Big Swede L.	LT,GR,WF,BB
7	16.8 Mile L.	LT,GR
8	Rusty L.	LT,GR
9	17-Mile L.	LT,GR
10	Denali-Clearwater Cr.	GR
11	Tangle Lakes	LT,GR,WF,BB
12	Rock Cr.	GR
13	Landmark Gap L.	LT,GR,WF
14	Glacier L.	LT,GR,WF
15	Boulder (7-Mile) L.	LT,GR,WF
16	36-Mile L.	LT,GR,WF
17	46.9-Mile	GR
18	Crooked Cr.	GR
19	50-Mile L.	GR,WF
20	Denali-Clearwater Cr.	GR
21	Butte Cr.	GR,WF

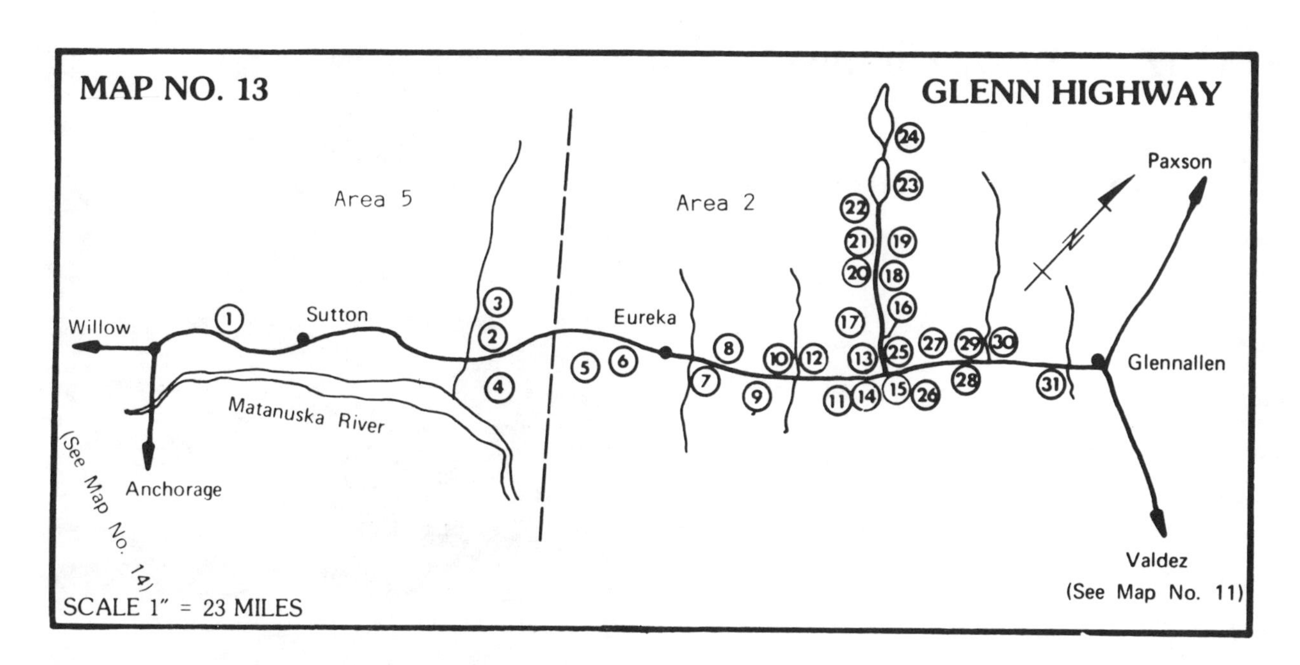
MAP NO. 13
GLENN HIGHWAY
Area 5
Area 2
Paxson
Willow
Sutton
Eureka
Glennallen
Matanuska River
Anchorage
(See Map No. 14)
Valdez
(See Map No. 11)
SCALE 1" = 23 MILES
1
2
3
4
5
6
7
8
9
10
11
12
13
14
15
16
17
18
19
20
21
22
23
24
25
26
27
28
29
30
31

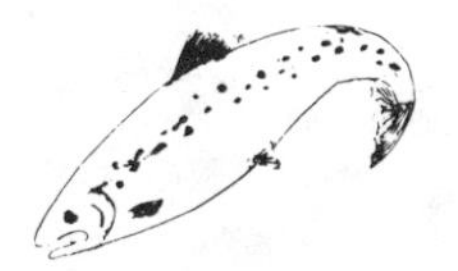

MAP NO. 13 GLENN HIGHWAY

KEY NO.	WATERWAYS	FISH SPECIES
1	Seventeen-Mile Lake	GR
2	Ravine Lake	RT
3	Lower Bonnie Lake	RT, GR
4	Long Lake	GR
5	Liela Lake	GR, BB
6	Gunsight Creek	GR
7	Cache Creek	GR
8	Alabama Lake	GR
9	Mirror Lake	GR
10	Mendeltna Creek	GR
11	Gergie Lake	GR
12	Sucker Lake	BB, GR
13	Buffalo Lake	RB
14	Arizona Lake	GR
15	Lake Louise Road	
16	Junction Lake	GR, SS
17	Crater Lake	RT
18	40-Foot Lake	GR
19	Peanut Lake	SS
20	Elbow Lake	GR
21	Caribou Lake	GR
22	George Lake	GR
23	Lake Louise	LT, WF, GR, BB
24	Susitna Lake	LT, WF, GR, BB
25	Tex Smith Lake	SS, RT
26	Lost Cabin Lake	GR
27	Kay Lake	GR
28	Mae West Lake	GR
29	Tolsona-Moose Lakes	GR, BB
30	Tolsona Creek	GR
31	Moose Creek	GR

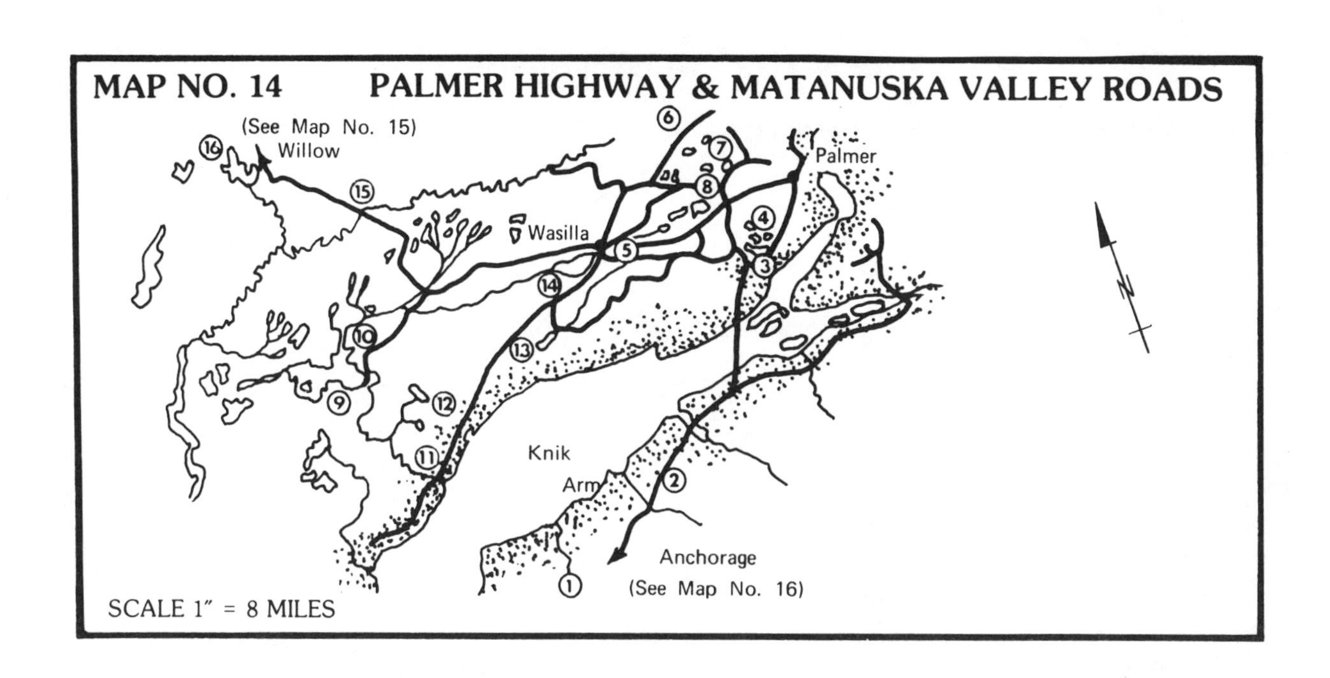
MAP NO. 14
PALMER HIGHWAY & MATANUSKA VALLEY ROADS
(See Map No. 15)
Willow
Palmer
Wasilla
Knik
Arm
Anchorage
(See Map No. 16)
SCALE 1" = 8 MILES
N

MAP NO. 14 PALMER HIGHWAY AND MATANUSKA VALLEY ROADS

KEY NO.	WATERWAY	FISH SPECIES
1	Lower Fire Lake	RT, DV, SS
2	Mirror (Bear) Lake	RT, SS
3	Echo Lake	RT
4	Kepler-Bradley Lake Complex	
	Kepler Lake	RT
	Bradley Lake	RT
	Victor Lake	SS, RT
	Irene Lake	RT
	Canoe Lake	RT, GR
	Long Lake	RT
5	Wasilla Lake	RT, SS
6	Reed Lake	RT, GR
7	Cornelius Lake	RT, SS, RS, DV
8	Finger Lake	SS
9	Big Lake	BB, RT, DV, SS, RS
10	Rocky Lake	SS
11	Fish Creek	RT, SS, RS, DV
12	Knik Lake	RT
13	Cottonwood Creek	RT, SS, RS
14	Lake Lucille	SS
15	Little Susitna River	DV, RT, SS, PS, CS
16	Nancy Lake Recreation Area	RT, DV, BB, WF,

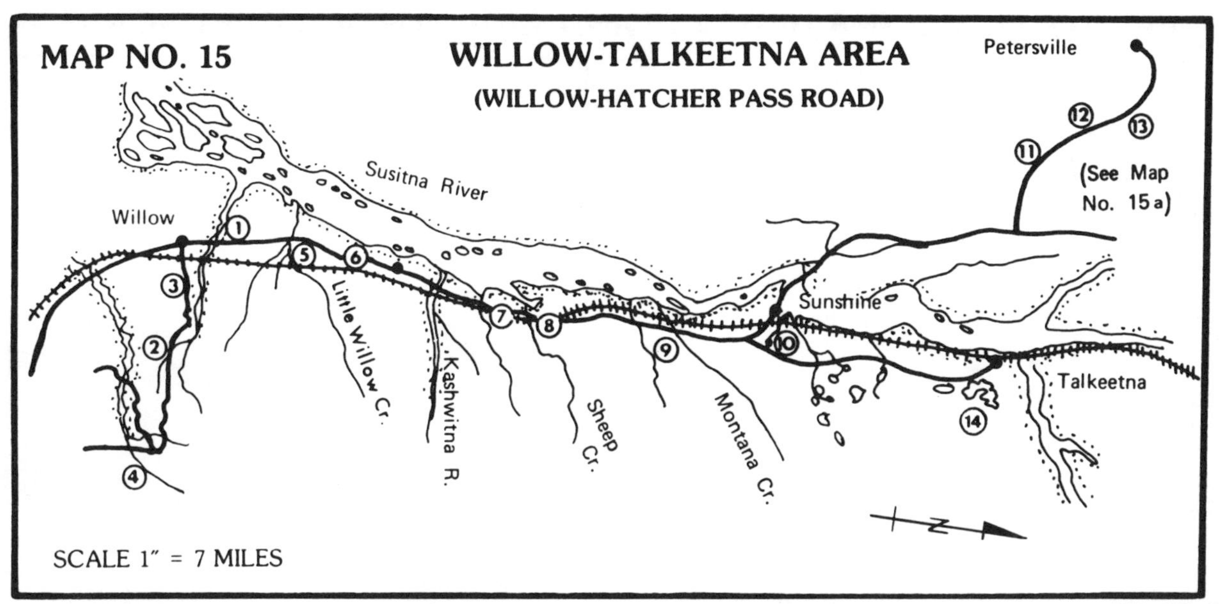

KEY NO.	WATERWAY	FISH SPECIES
1	Lower Willow Creek (Below Canyon Rapids)	RT, GR, DV, SS, CS, PS
2	Upper Willow Creek (Above Canyon Rapids)	DV
3	Deception Creek	RT, DV, SS, PS, CS
4	Upper Little Susitna River	DV
5	Little Willow Creek	RT, GR, SS, PS
6	Kashwitna Lake	SS
7	Caswell Creek	RT, GR, SS, PS, CS
8	Sheep Creek	RT, GR, DV, WF, SS, PS, CS
9	Montana Creek	RT, GR, DV, WF, SS, PS, CS
10	Birch Creek	RT, WF, SS, RS
11	Moose Creek	RT, GR, SS, KS
12	Kroto Creek	RT, GR, SS, KS
13	Martin Creek	GR
14	Christiansen Lake	SS

ALASKA BUSH CARRIER

Fly with the guys who know the skies of Alaska

FISHING
HUNTING
CAMPING

Float Trips

243-3127

4801 Aircraft Drive, Anchorage, Alaska

West Lakeshore of
(LAKE HOOD)

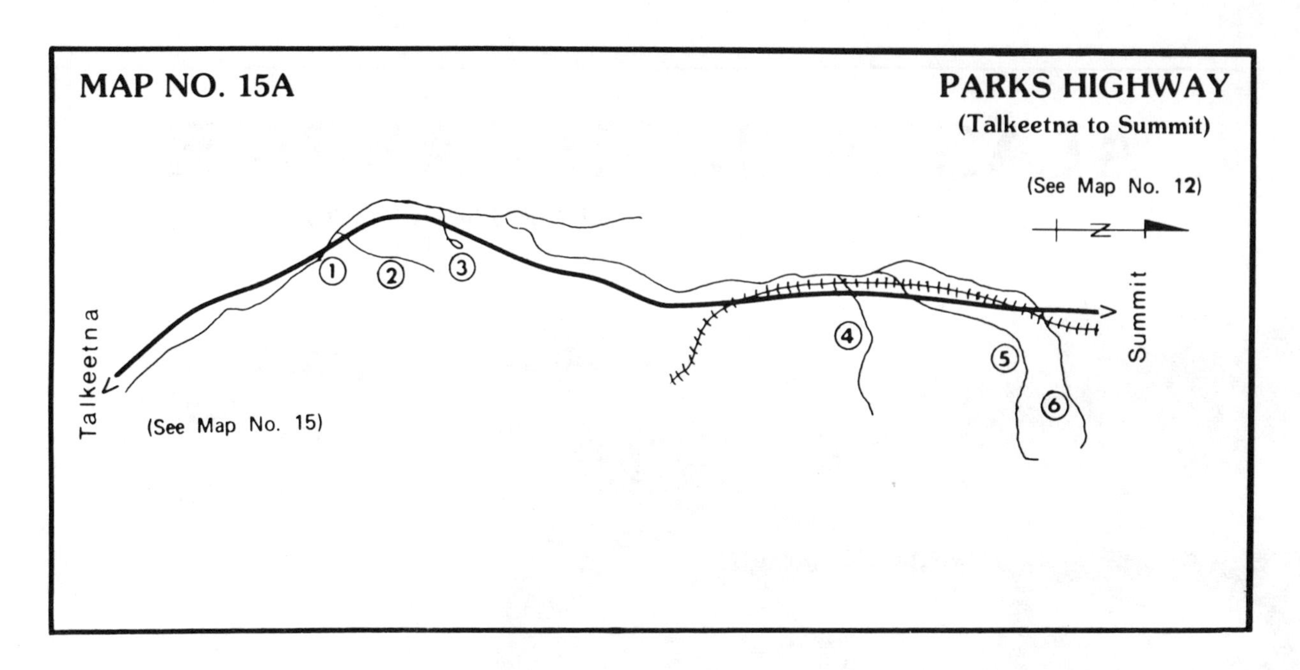

KEY NO.	WATERWAY	FISH SPECIES
1	Chulitna River	RT, GR, WF
2	Troublesome Creek	GR
3	Byers Lake	LT, BB, WF
4	Honolulu Creek	GR
5	East Fork, Chulitna River	RT, GR, WF
6	Middle Fork, Chulitna River	RT, GR, WF

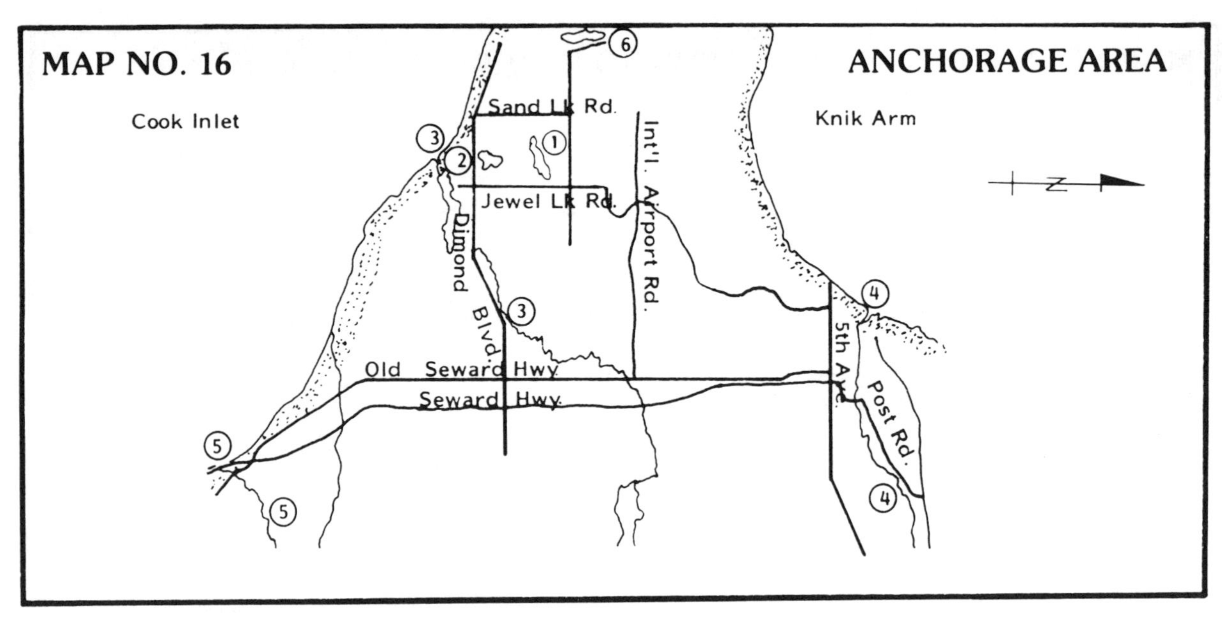

KEY NO.	WATERWAY	FISH SPECIES
1	Sand Lake	RT
2	Jewel Lake	RT
3	Campbell Creek	DV, SS, PS
4	Ship Creek	SS, KS, PS, CS, DV
5	Rabbit Creek	PS, DV
6	Campbell Pt. Lake	RT

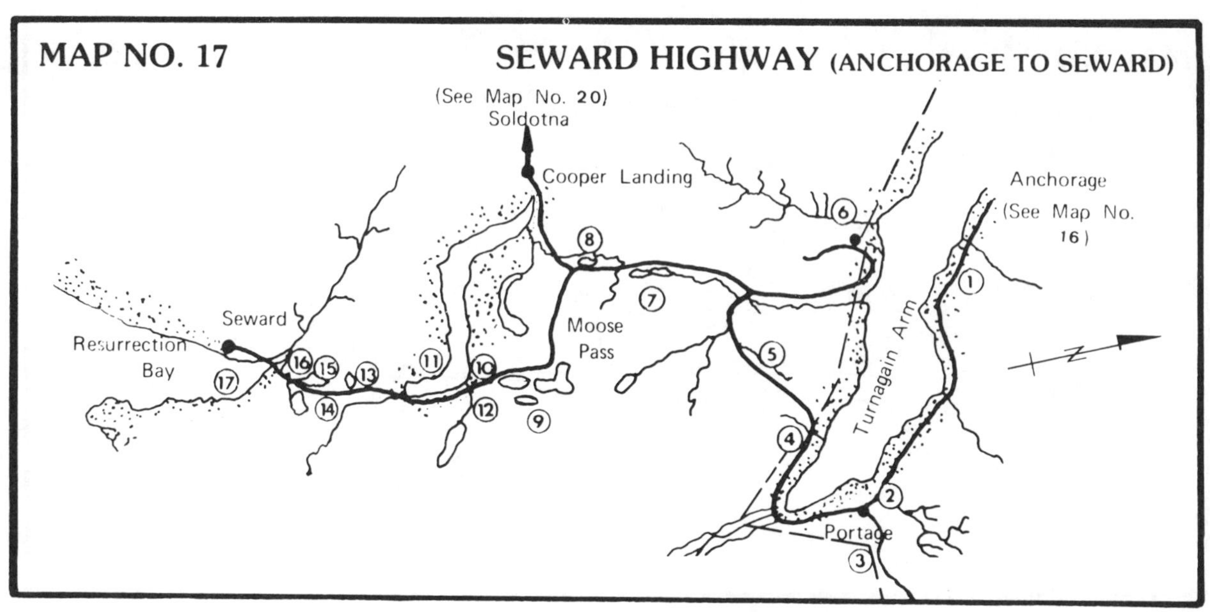

KEY NO.	WATERWAY	FISH SPECIES
1	Bird Creek	DV, PS
2	Twenty-Mile River	SS, Smelt
3	Portage Creek	RS, DV, SS
4	Ingram Creek	PS, DV
5	Granite Creek	DV
6	Resurrection Creek	PS, DV
7	Summit Lakes	DV
8	Jerome Lake	RT, DV
9	Vagt Lake	RT
10	Trail River	DV, RT, LT
11	Kenai Lake	RT, DV, LT, WF
12	Ptarmigan Creek	RT, DV
13	Grayling Lake	GR
14	Goldenfin Lake	DV
15	Grouse Lake	DV
16	Salmon Creek	DV
17	Resurrection Bay	SS, PS, DV, Bottomfish

SILVER SALMON AND
HALIBUT FISHING
CHARTERS
FISHING TACKLE LICENSES
MARINE SUPPLIES
SPORTING GOODS ICE & BAIT
EVENRUDE MOTORS & PARTS
THE
FISH
HOUSE
FISH HOUSE
BOX 1345
SEWARD
ALASKA
224-3674
DAILY SIGHTSEEING
TOURS TO KENAI FJORDS
NAT'L PARK

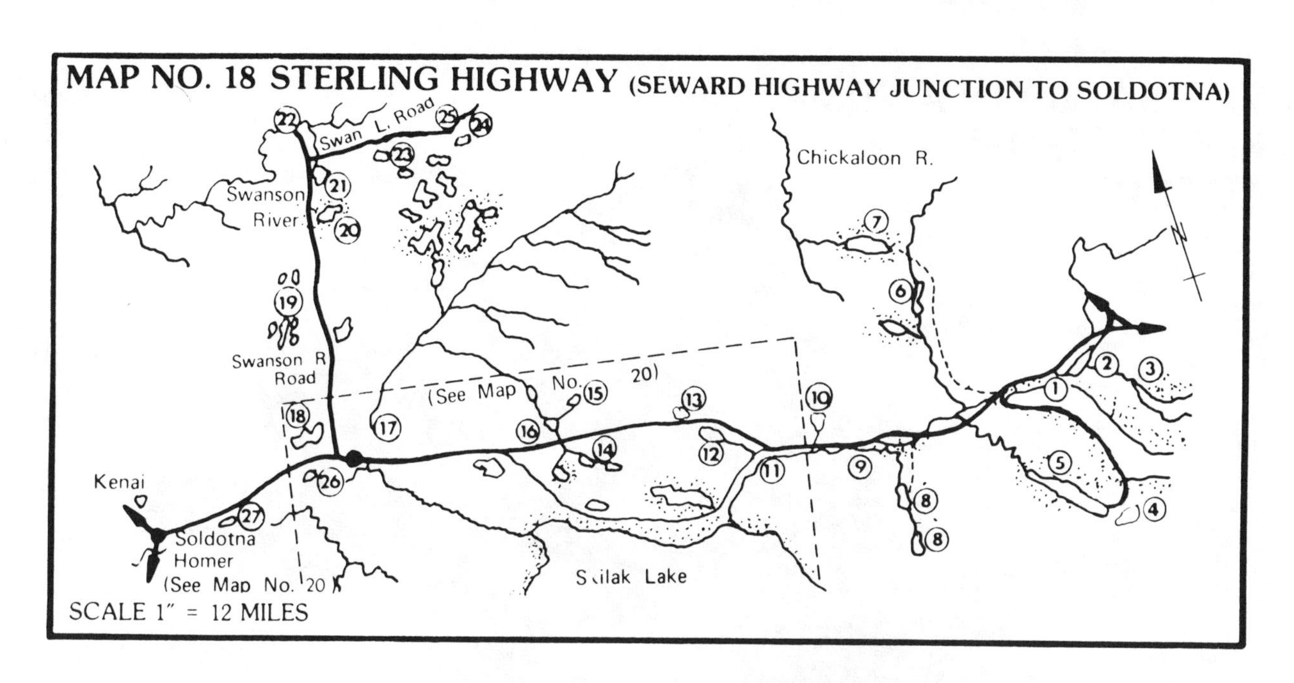
MAP NO. 18 STERLING HIGHWAY (SEWARD HIGHWAY JUNCTION TO SOLDOTNA)
Swan L. Road
Chickaloon R.
Swanson River
Swanson R Road
(See Map No. 20)
Kenai
Soldotna
Homer
(See Map No. 20)
Skilak Lake
SCALE 1" = 12 MILES

MAP NO. 18 STERLING HIGHWAY

KEY NO.	WATERWAY	FISH SPECIES
1	Quartz Creek	RT, DV
2	Crescent Creek	GR
3	Crescent Lake	GR
4	Rainbow Lake	RT
5	Cooper Lake	DV
6	Juneau Lake	RT, LT, WF
7	Swan Lake	RT, LT, DV, RS
8	Russian Lakes	RT, DV
9	Russian River	RT, DV, RS, SS
10	South Fuller Lake	GR
11	Skilak Loop Road	
12	Jean Lake	RT, DV
13	Upper Jean Lake	SS
14	Kelly and Peterson Lakes	RT
15	Watson Lake	RT
16	East Fork of Moose River	RT
17	Moose River	RT, DV, RS
18	Sunken Island Lake	SS
19	Forest Lakes	RT
20	Dolly Varden Lake	RT, AC
21	Rainbow Trout Lake	RT, AC
22	Swanson River	RT, DV, SS
23	Swan Lake Canoe Portage System	RT, AC
24	Portage Lake	SS
25	Swanson River Canoe Portage System	RT, AC, SS
26	Scout Lake	SS
27	Longmare Lake	RT

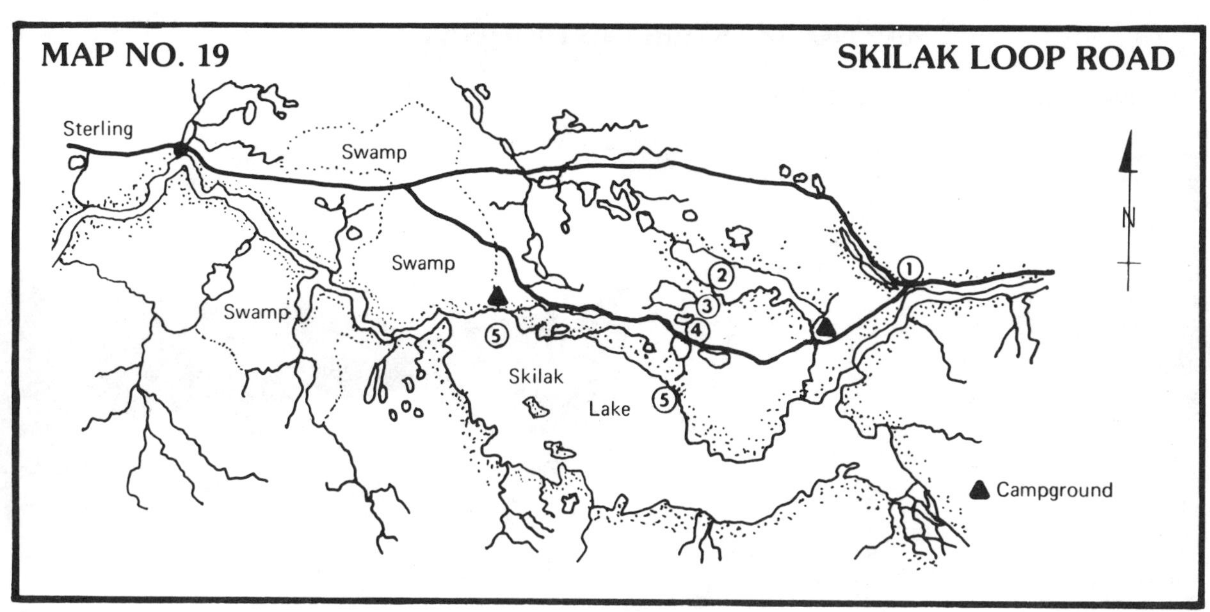

KEY NO.	WATERWAY	FISH SPECIES
1	East Entrance of Skilak Loop Road	
2	Hidden Lake	RT, DV
3	Engineer Lake	SS
4	Ohmer Lakes	RT, DV
5	Skilak Lake	RT, LT, DV, SS, WF

CHARTER

ALORA CHARTERS

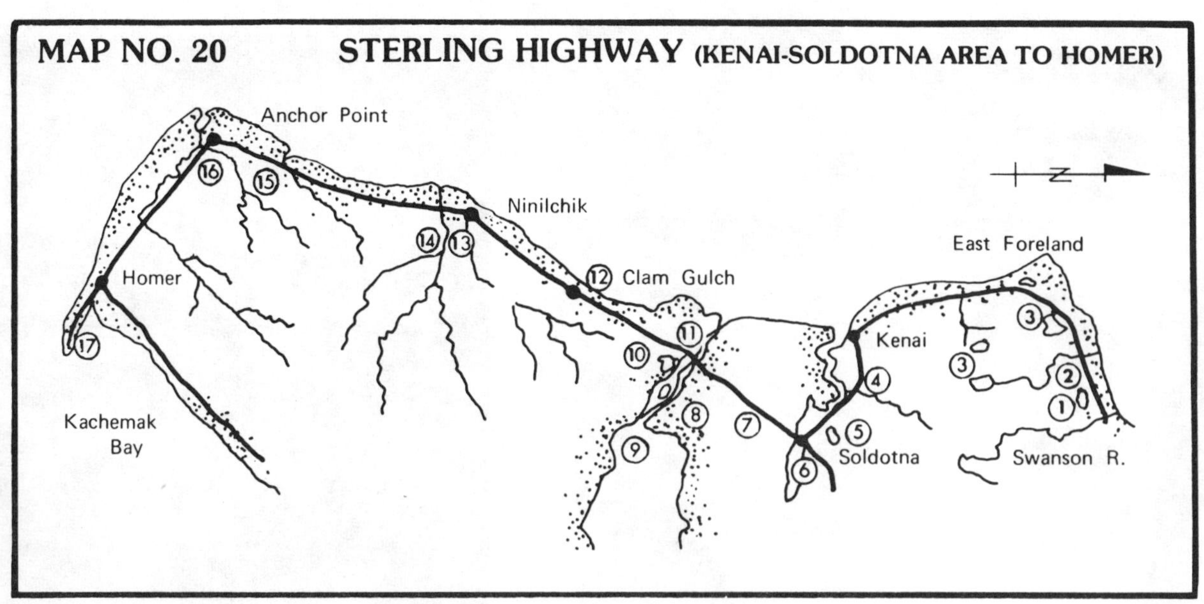

MAP NO. 20 STERLING HIGHWAY (KENAI-SOLDOTNA AREA TO HOMER)

KEY NO.	WATERWAY	FISH SPECIES
1	Stormy Lake	AC, RT
2	Bishop Creek	RT
3	Cabin Lake	RT
4	Beaver Creek	RT, DV
5	Sport Lake	RT
6	Kenai River	RT, DV, SS, PS, RS, KS
7	Arc Lake	SS
8	Centennial Lake	SS
9	Tustumena Lake	LT, DV, WF, SS
10	Johnson Lake	RT
11	Crooked Creek	RT, DV
12	Clam Gulch	Razor Clams
13	Ninilchik River	DV, SH, KS, SS
14	Deep Creek	DV, SH, KS, SS
15	Stariski Creek	DV, SH, SS
16	Anchor River	DV, SH, KS, SS
17	Homer Spit	DV, SS, PS, H, Bottomfish

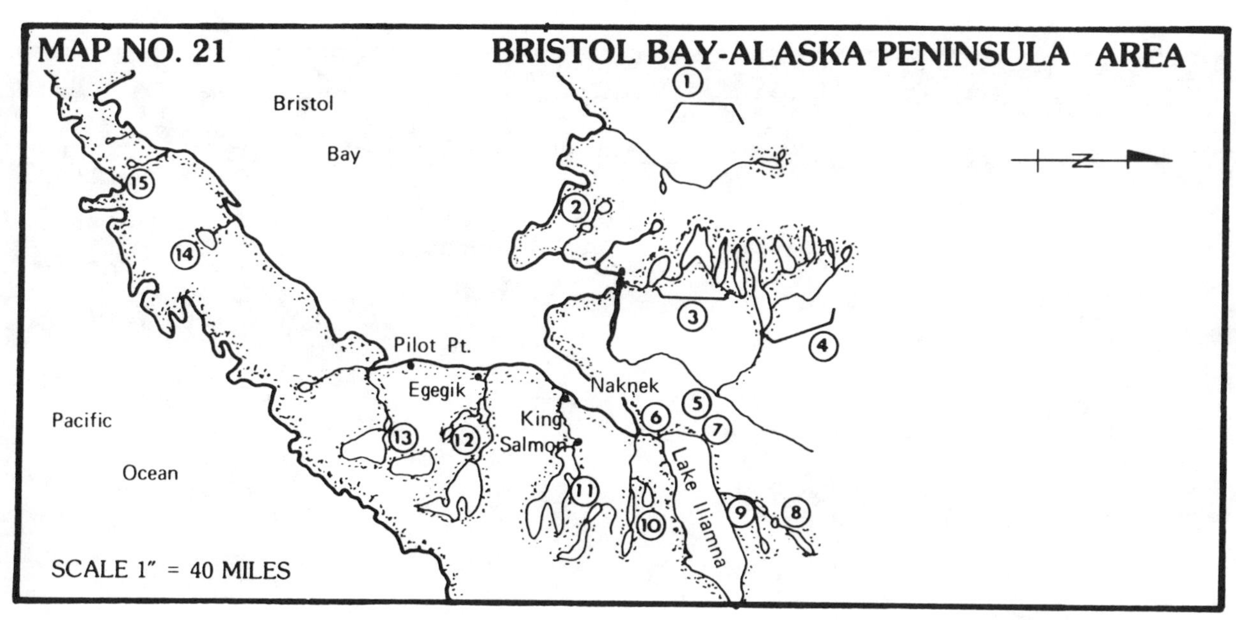
MAP NO. 21
BRISTOL BAY-ALASKA PENINSULA AREA
Bristol
Bay
Pilot Pt.
Egegik
Naknek
King
Salmon
Lake Iliamna
Pacific
Ocean
SCALE 1" = 40 MILES
N
1
2
3
4
5
6
7
8
9
10
11
12
13
14
15

MAP NO. 21 BRISTOL BAY-ALASKA PENINSULA AREA

KEY NO.	WATERWAY	FISH SPECIES
1	Togiak River System	
	Togiak River	KS, SS, PS, GR, AC
	Togiak Lake (outlet)	GR, AC
	Ongivinuk Lake (outlet)	RT, GR, AC
	Gechiak Lake (outlet)	RT, GR, AC, SS
	Pungokepuk Lake (outlet)	RT, GR, NP
2	Igushik River System	
	Igushik River	RT, GR, AC
	Amanka Lake	GR, AC
	Kathlene River (mouth)	GR, AC
3	Wood River System	
	Wood River	DS, PS, RT, GR, AC
	Lake Aleknagik (outlet)	RT, AC, RS
	Agulowak (2nd river)	RT, GR, AC, RS
	Agulukpuk (3rd river)	RT, GR, NP, AC, RS
	Lynx Creek (Lake Nerka)	RT, GR, AC
	Little Togiak River (Lake Nerka)	RT, GR, AC
	Peace River (4th river)	GR, AC
	Wind River (5th river)	RT, GR, AC
	Grant River (6th river)	RT, GR, AC, NP
4	Tikchik Lake System	
	Nuyakuk River	RT, GR, AC, NP, SS, KS, PS, RS
	Tikchik Lake (outlet)	RT, GR, LT, AC
	Nuyakuk-Tikchik Narrows	LT, GR, AC
	Chauekuktuli-Nuyakuk Narrows	GR, NP
	Allen River	GR
5	Nushagak River System	
	Nushagak River-Mulchatna	RT, GR, DV, CS
	Portage Creek (mouth)	PS, KS, NP
	Klutuk Creek	KS, SS
	Koktuli River	KS
	Old Stuyahok River	RT, KS
	King Salmon River	KS
6	Kvichak River System	
	Iguigig-Kaskanak	RT, GR, DV, RS, CS
7	Lower Talarik Creek	RT, GR, NP, RS, SS
8	Lake Clark	LT, NP, RS
9	Newhalen River System	
	Copper River	RT, DV, GR, RS
	Gibraltar Lake	GR
	Iliamna River	RT, GR, DV, RS
10	Alagnak (Branch) River System	
	Kukaklek Lake (outlet)	RT, GR, AC
	Battle River	RT, LT, RS
	Funnel Creek	RT, KS
	Nonvianuk Lake (outlet)	RT, AC, LT
	Kulik River	RT
11	Naknek Watershed	
	Naknek River	RT, GR, DV, KS, SS, PS, RS, CS

MAP NO. 21 BRISTOL BAY-ALASKA PENINSULA (Continued)

KEY NO.	WATERWAY	FISH SPECIES
	Naknek Watershed (Continued)	
	King Salmon Creek	RT, GR, DV, KS, SS, CS
	Big Creek	RT, GR, DV, KS, SS, CS
	Brooks River	RT, GR, DV, RS
	Idavain Lake	DV
	Naknek Lake	RT, AC, LT, NP
	Colville-Grosvenor Narrows	RT, GR, DV, LT, NP
	American Creek	RT, GR, DV, RS
12	Egegik River System	
	Becharof Lake (outlet)	GR, AC, RS
	Ruth River	GR, AC, RS
	Featherly Creek & others	GR, AC, RS
13	Ugashik River System	
	Lower Ugashik Lake (outlet)	GR, AC, SS, RS
	Narrows between lakes	GR, LT, AC, DV, SS
	Meshik River	GR, DV, KS, SS
	Mother Goose Lake (outlet)	GR, DV, KS, SS
14	Sandy River System	DV, AC, KS, SS
15	Bear River System	DV, AC, KS, SS

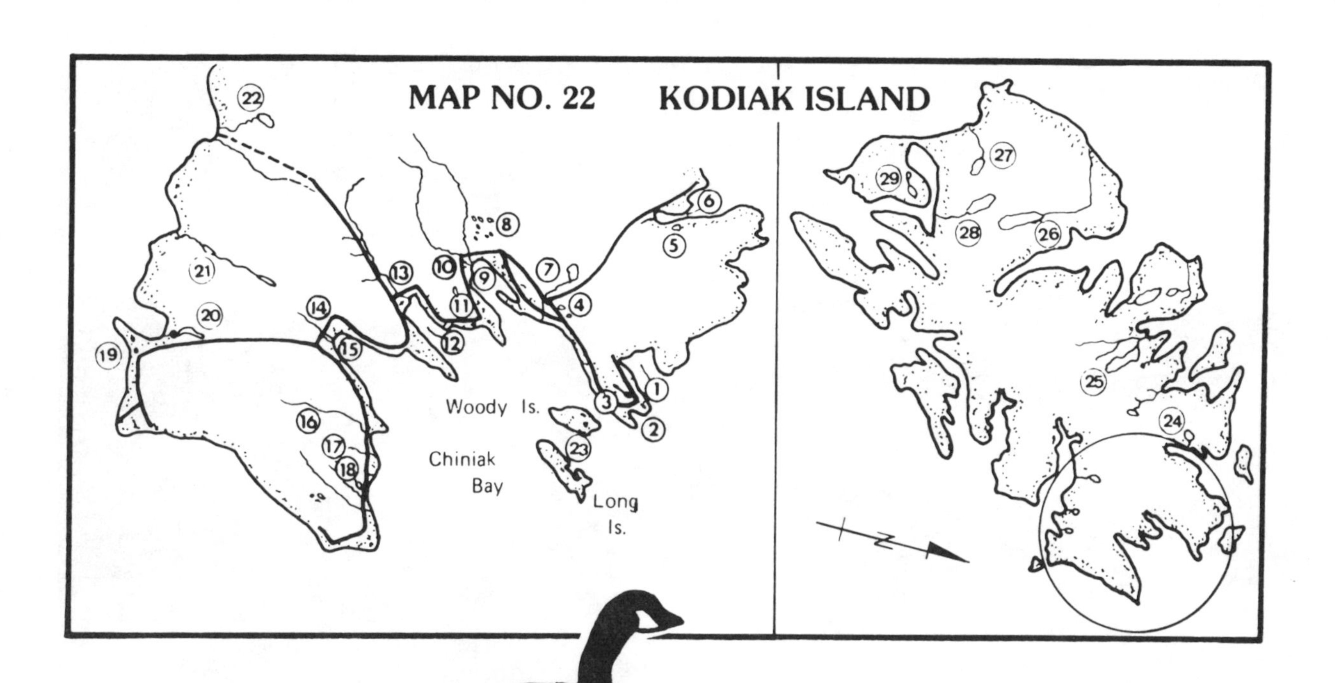

MAP NO. 22
KODIAK ISLAND
Woody Is.
Chiniak
Bay
Long
Is.
1
2
3
4
5
6
7
8
9
10
11
12
13
14
15
16
17
18
19
20
21
22
23
24
25
26
27
28
29

MAP NO. 22 KODIAK ISLAND (Continued)

KEY NO.	WATERWAY	FISH SPECIES
1	Monashka Bay	DV, RF, SS, PS, Greenling, H
2	Ambercrombie Lake	RT, GR
3	Island and Dark Lakes	RT, DV
4	Genevieve & Margaret Lakes	RT
5	Cascade Lake	RT, GR
6	Anton Larsen Bay	SS, PS, CS, DV, H, Crab
7	Buskin River	DV, PS, SS, RS, CS, H, Crab
8	Womens Bay	DV, PS, SS
9	**Bell's Flat Lakes**	RT, GR, DV
10	Russian River	DV, PS, CS
11	Cliff Point Lakes	RT
12	Middle Bay	CS, PS, SS, DV, H, Crab, Clams
13	American River	SS, PS, CS, DV
14	**Olds River and Kalsin River**	DV, SS, PS
15	Kalsin Bay	PS, SS, DV
16	Roslyn River and beach	PS, DV, SS
17	Twin Forks & Chiniak Creeks	DV, PS, SS
18	Pony Lake	SS, DV
19	Pasagshak Pt. lakes	RT
20	Lake Rose Tead and Pasagshak River	DV, SS, PS, RS
21	**Lake Miam**	**RT, SH, PS, SS, DV, RS**
22	Saltery Lake and River	RT, SH, RS, PS, SS, DV
23	Woody & Long Island lakes	RT, SS, DV, GR

KODIAK WILDLIFE REFUGE

KEY NO.	WATERWAY	FISH SPECIES
24	Barbara Lake	RT, DV, RS, SS
25	Uganik Lake & River	RT, SH, DV, RS, PS, SS
26	Karluk Lake, River & Lagoon	RT, SH, DV, RS, PS, SS, KS
27	Red Lake & River	RT, SH, DV, RS, PS, SS, KS
28	Upper Station Lakes	RT, SH, DV, PS, RS, SS
29	Akalura Lake	RT, SH, DV, SS, RS, PS

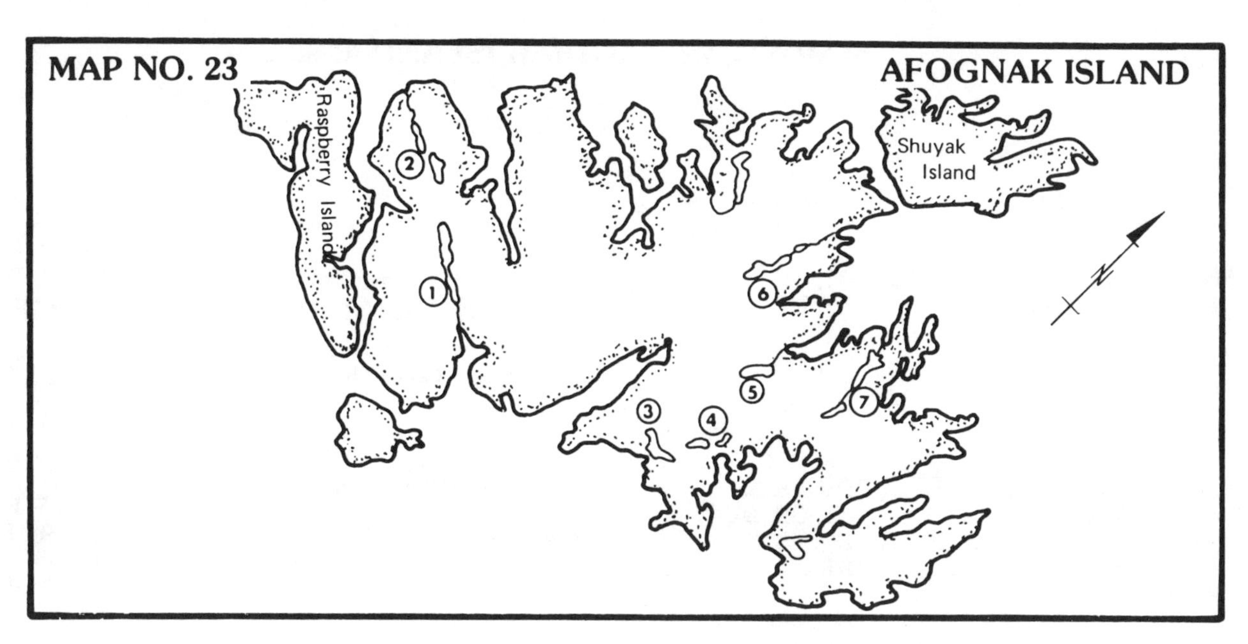

KEY NO.	WATERWAY	FISH SPECIES
1	Afognak Lake and River	RT, SH, DV, RS, PS, SS
2	Malina Lakes	RT, SH, DV, RS, PS, SS
3	Little Afognak Lake	RT, SH, DV, RS, SS
4	Kitoi Lakes	RT, DV, SS, RS
5	Portage Lake	RT, SH, DV, RS, PS, SS
6	Waterfall Lake	DV
7	Pauls-Laura Lake	RT, SH, DV, RS, PS, SS

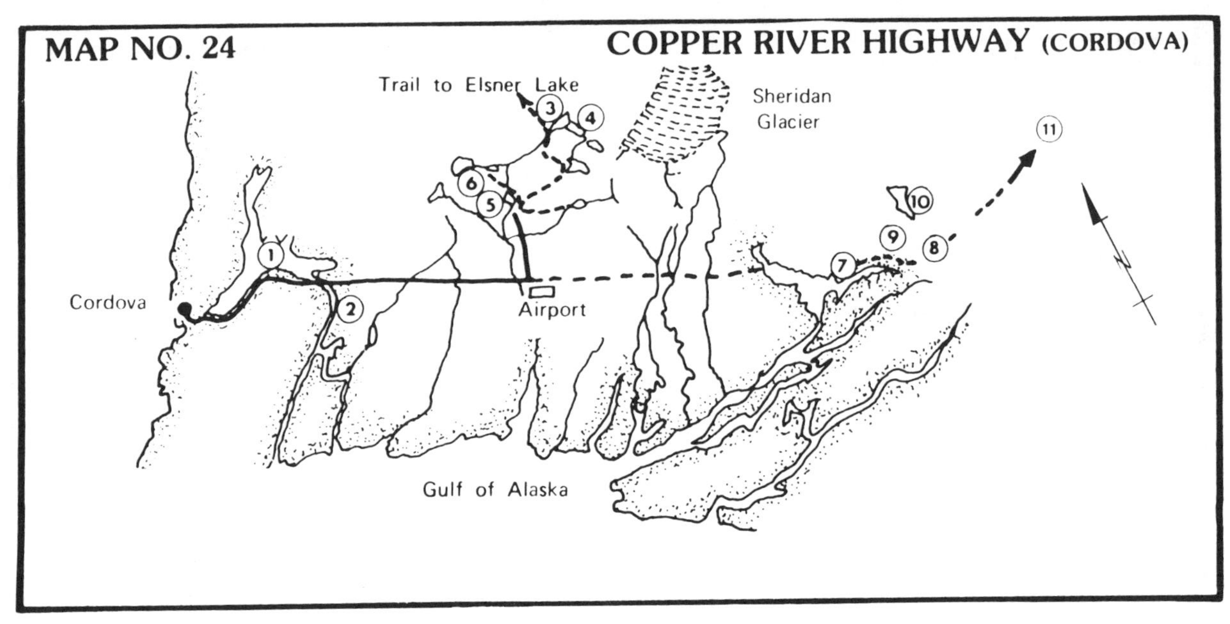

KEY NO.	WATERWAY	FISH SPECIES
1	Eyak Lake	SS, RS, CT
2	Eyak River	SS, RS, CT
3	Beaver Lake	DV, CT
4	Upper Beaver Lake	DV, CT
5	Cabin Lake	CT
6	Island Lake	CT
7	19-Mile Lake	DV, CT
8	Pipeline Lake	GR, DV, CT
9	22-Mile Lake	DV, CT
10	McKinley Lake	DV, CT
11	Clear Creek	DV

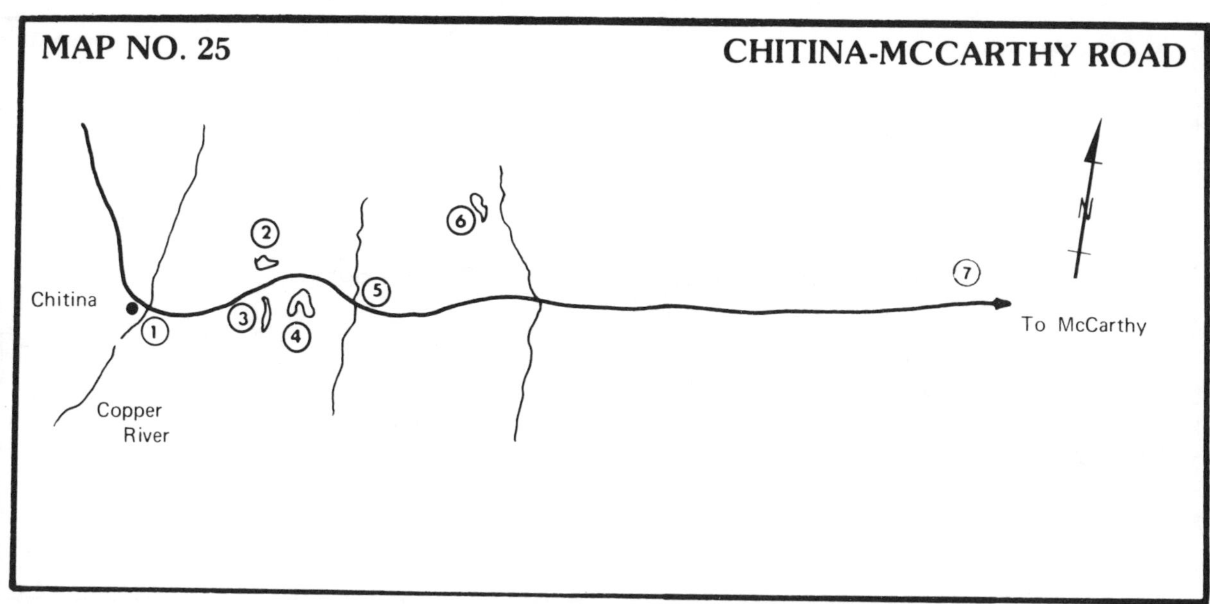

KEY NO.	WATERWAY	FISH SPECIES
1	Copper River	RS, KS
2	Strelna Lake	RT, SS
3	Van Lake	RT
4	Sculpin Lake	RT
5	Strelna Creek	DV
6	Lou's Lake	SS, GR
7	Long Lake	GR, BB, LT, SS, DV

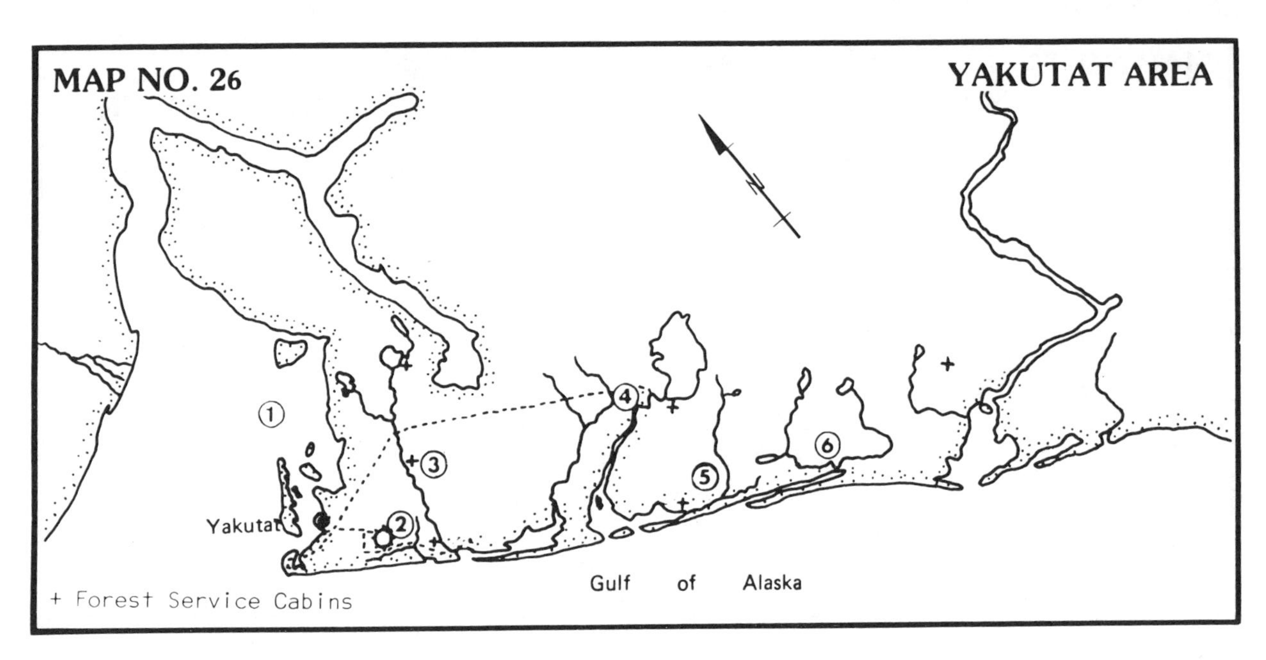

KEY NO.	WATERWAY	FISH SPECIES
1	Yakutat Bay	KS, SS, H
2	Lost River	SS, DV
3	Situk River	SH, SS, DV, KS, RS, PS, Smelt
4	Ahrnklin River	SS, RS, DV
5	Italio River	SS, DT, DV, Smelt
6	Akwe River	KS, SS, RS, CT, DV

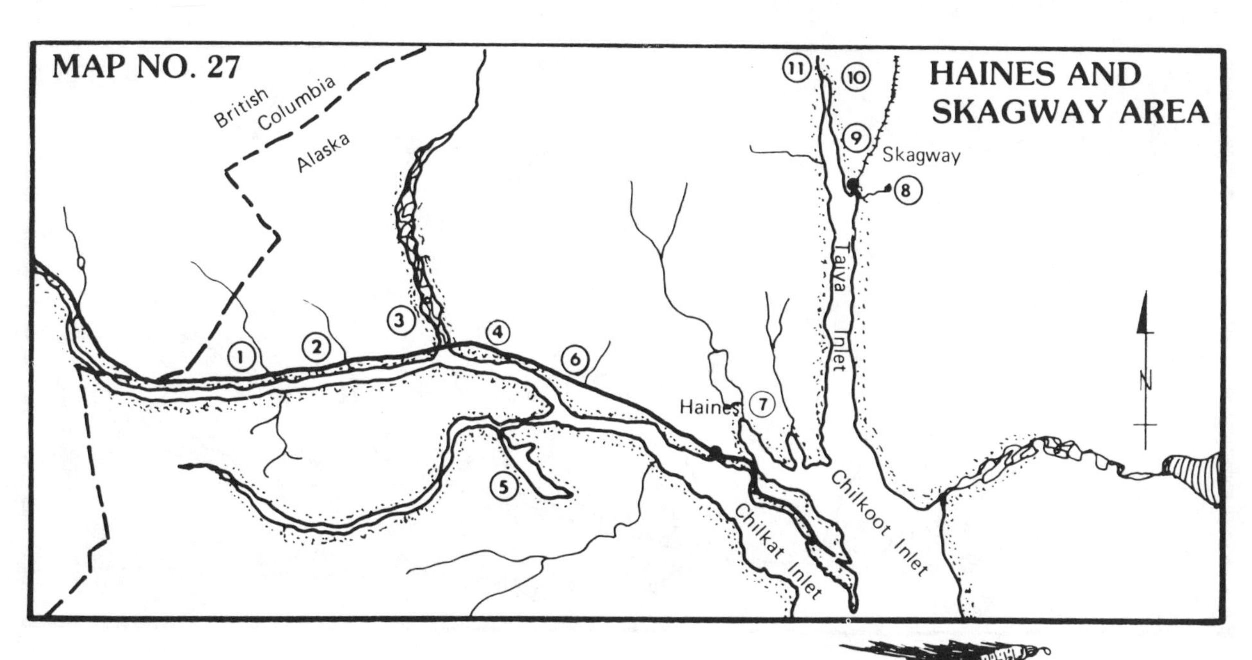

KEY NO.	WATERWAY	FISH SPECIES
1	Big Boulder Creek	DV
2	31-Mile Slough	DV, CS, SS
3	Mosquito Lake	DV, CT, WF
4	Chilkat River	CT, DV, CS, SS, PS
5	Chilkat Lake	WF, DV
6	14-Mile Slough	DV, CS, SS, PS
7	Chilkoot Lake outlet	RS, PS, DV, SS
8	Lower Dewey Lake	RT, BT
9	Black Lake	DV
10	Dyea Slough	DV, PS, CS, SS
11	Lost Lake	RT

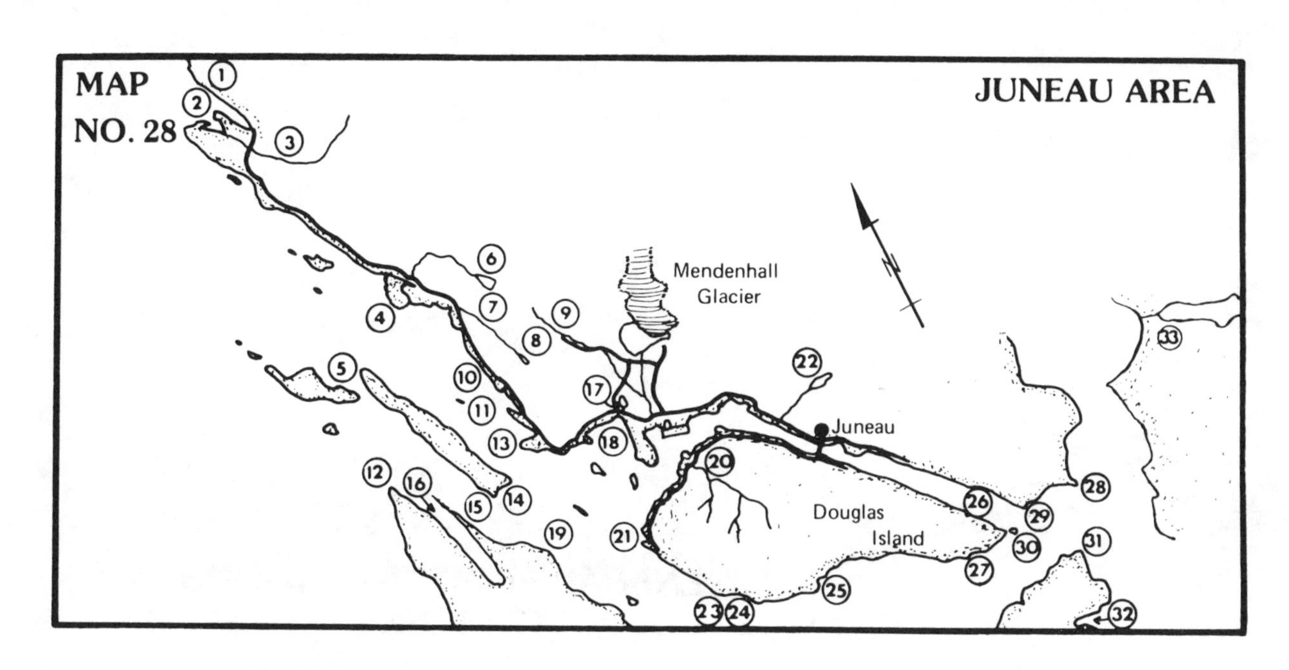
MAP
NO. 28
JUNEAU AREA
Mendenhall
Glacier
Juneau
Douglas
Island
1
2
3
4
5
6
7
8
9
10
11
12
13
14
15
16
17
18
19
20
21
22
23
24
25
26
27
28
29
30
31
32
33

MAP NO. 28 JUNEAU AREA (Continued)

KEY NO.	WATERWAY	FISH SPECIES
1	Antler Lake	GR (to 18")
2	Echo Cove	DV, CT, KS, SS, CS, PS, H
3	Cowee Creek	DV, CT, SS, CS, PS
4	Eagle River	DV, SS
5	North Pass	KS, SS, PS, CS, DV, H, RF
6	Windfall Lake	DV, CT, SS, RS
7	Peterson Creek	DV, CT, SH, SS, CS, PS
8	Peterson Lake	DV, RT
9	Montana Creek	DV, CT, SS, CS, PS
10	The Breadline	KS, SS, PS, CS DV, H, RF
11	Aaron Island	KS, SS, PS, CS, DV, H, RF
12	Point Retreat	KS, SS, PS, CS, DV, H, RF
13	Lena Point	KS, SS, PS, CS, DV, H, RF
14	South Shelter Island	KS, SS, PS, CS DV, H, RF
15	Favorite Reef	KS, SS, PS, CS, DV, H, RF
16	Barlow Cove	KS, SS, PS, CS, DV, H, RF
17	Auke Lake and Creek	DV, CT, SS, CS, PS, RS
18	Auke Bay	KS, SS, PS, CS, RS, DV, H, RF
19	Piling Point	KS, SS, PS, CS, DV, H, RF
20	Fish Creek	DV, CT, CS, PS
21	Outer Point	KS, SS, PS, CS, DV, H, RF
22	Salmon Creek Res.	BT
23	Middle Point	KS, SS, PS, CS, DV, H, RF
24	White Marker	KS, SS, PS, CS, DV, H, RF
25	Point Hilda	KS, SS, PS, CS, DV, H, RF
26	Dupont	KS, SS, PS, CS, DV, H, RF
27	Icy Point	KS, SS, PS, CS, DV, H, RF
28	Point Bishop	KS, SS, PS, CS, DV, H, RF
29	Point Salibury	KS, SS, PS, CS, DV, H, RF
30	Marmion Island	KS, SS, PS, CS, DV, H, RF
31	Point Arden	KS, SS, PS, CS, DV, H, RF
32	Doty Cove	KS, SS, PS, CS, DV, H, RF
33	Turner Lake	CT, DV

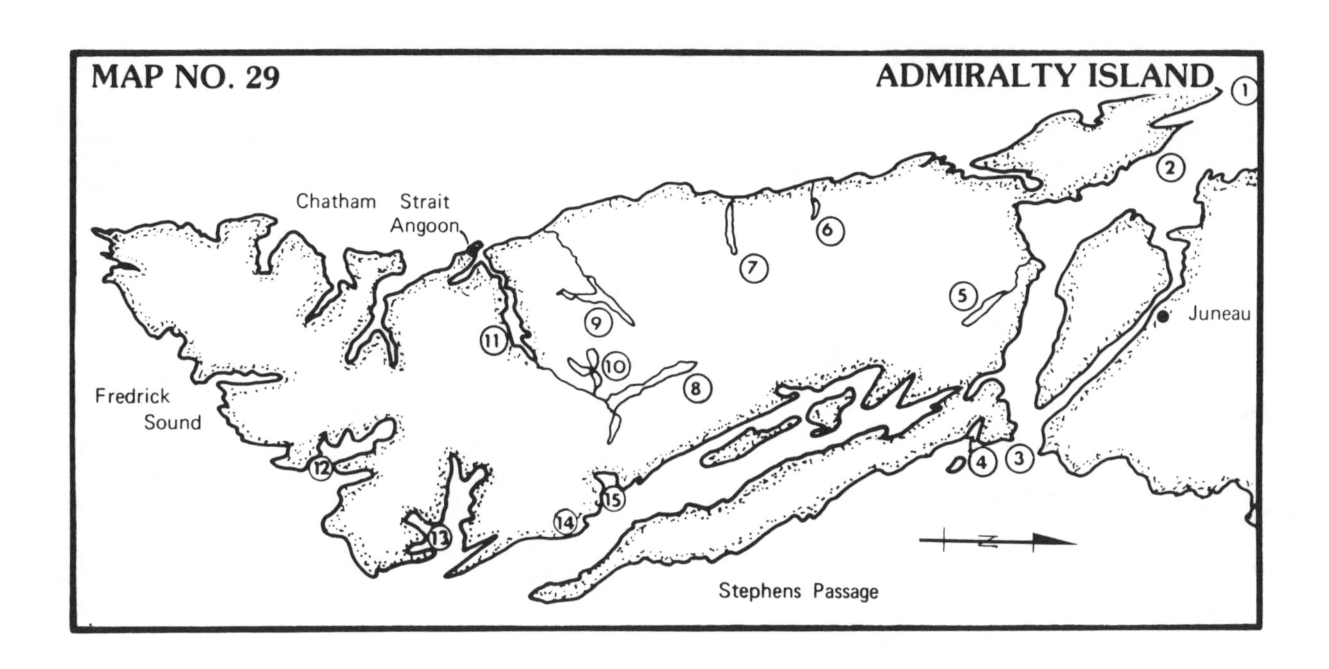
MAP NO. 29
ADMIRALTY ISLAND
Chatham Strait
Angoon
Fredrick Sound
Juneau
Stephens Passage
N
1
2
3
4
5
6
7
8
9
10
11
12
13
14
15

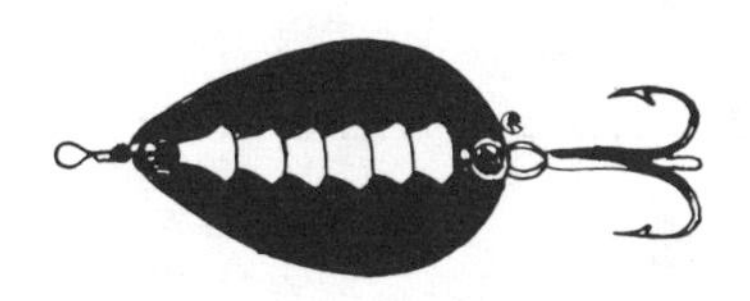

MAP NO. 29 ADMIRALTY ISLAND

KEY NO.	WATERWAY	FISH SPECIES
1	Point Retreat	KS, SS, PS, CS, RS, DV, H, RF
2	Piling Point	KS, SS, PS, CS, RS, DV, H, RF
3	Point Arden	KS, SS, PS, CS, RS, DV, H, RF
4	Doty Cove	KS, SS, PS, CS, RS, DV, H, RF
5	Youngs Lake	RT, SH, CT, DV, SS
6	Lake Kathleen	CT, DV
7	Lake Florence	CT, DV
8	Hasselborg Lake	CT, DV
9	Thayer Lake	CT, DV
10	Jims, Davidson, Distin, & Guerin Lakes	CT, DV
11	Mitchell Bay	CT, DV
12	Pybus Bay	KS, SS, H, DV, PS
13	Gambier Bay	KS, SS, H, DV, PS
14	Pleasant Bay Creek	DV, PS, SS, CT, SH
15	Mole Harbor	DV, PS, CS, SS, CT, SH

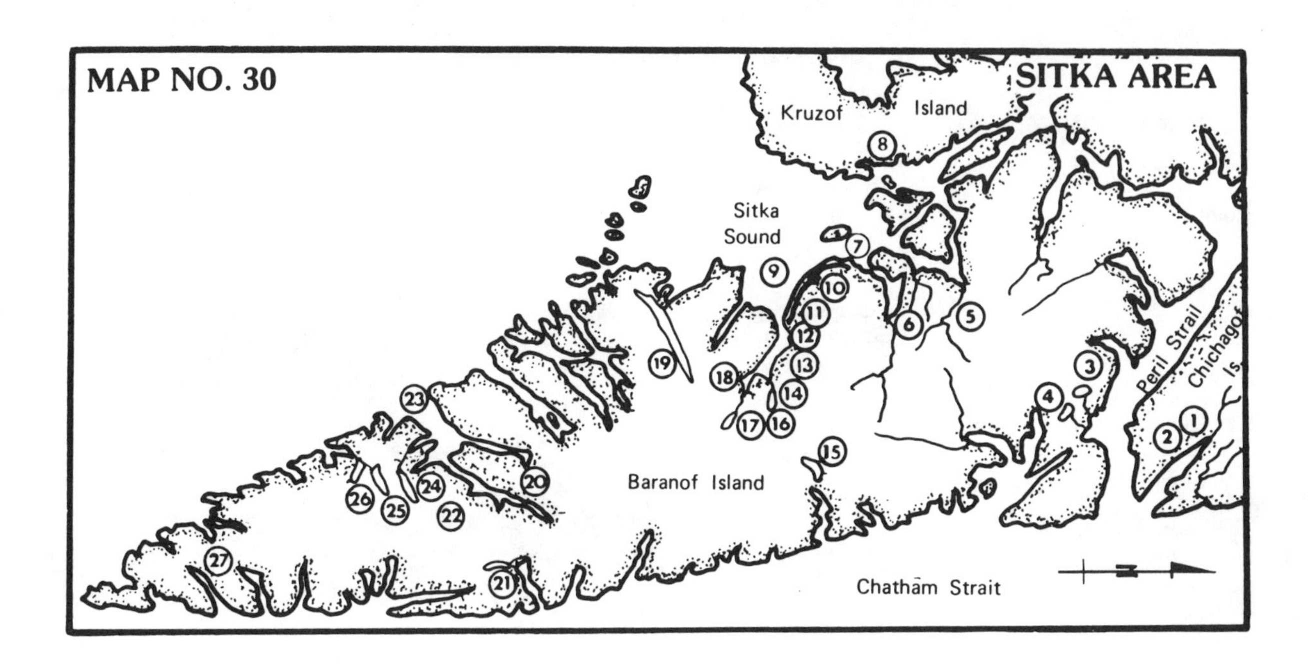
MAP NO. 30
SITKA AREA
Kruzof Island
Sitka Sound
Baranof Island
Peril Strait
Chichagof Is.
Chatham Strait
1
2
3
4
5
6
7
8
9
10
11
12
13
14
15
16
17
18
19
20
21
22
23
24
25
26
27

MAP NO. 30 SITKA AREA

KEY NO.	WATERWAY	FISH SPECIES
1	Sitkoh Lake	CT, SS
2	Sitkoh Creek	DV, SS, CT, SH, RS
3	Lake Eva	CT, DV
4	Little Lake Eva	CT
5	Nakwasina River	SS, Sea-run DV
6	Katlian River	DV, CT, SS, PS, CS
7	Starrigavin Bay	DV, PS, SS
8	Kamenoi Beach	Razor Clams
9	Sitka Sound	DV, KS, SS, LC, RF, H, PS
10	Swan Lake	RT
11	Thimbleberry Lake	BT
12	Heart Lake	BT
13	Blue Lake	RT
14	Beaver Lake	GR
15	Baranof Lake	CT
16	Medvejia Lake	DV
17	Green Lake	BT
18	Salmon Lake	CT, SH, SS, RS, DV, PS, CS
19	Redoubt Lake	DV, PS, CS, SS, RS
20	Avoss Lake	RT
21	Pass Lake	RT
22	Davidof Lake	RT
23	Port Banks	SS
24	Lake Plotnikof	RT
25	Khvostof Lake	RT
26	Rezanof Lake	RT
27	Gar Lake	RT

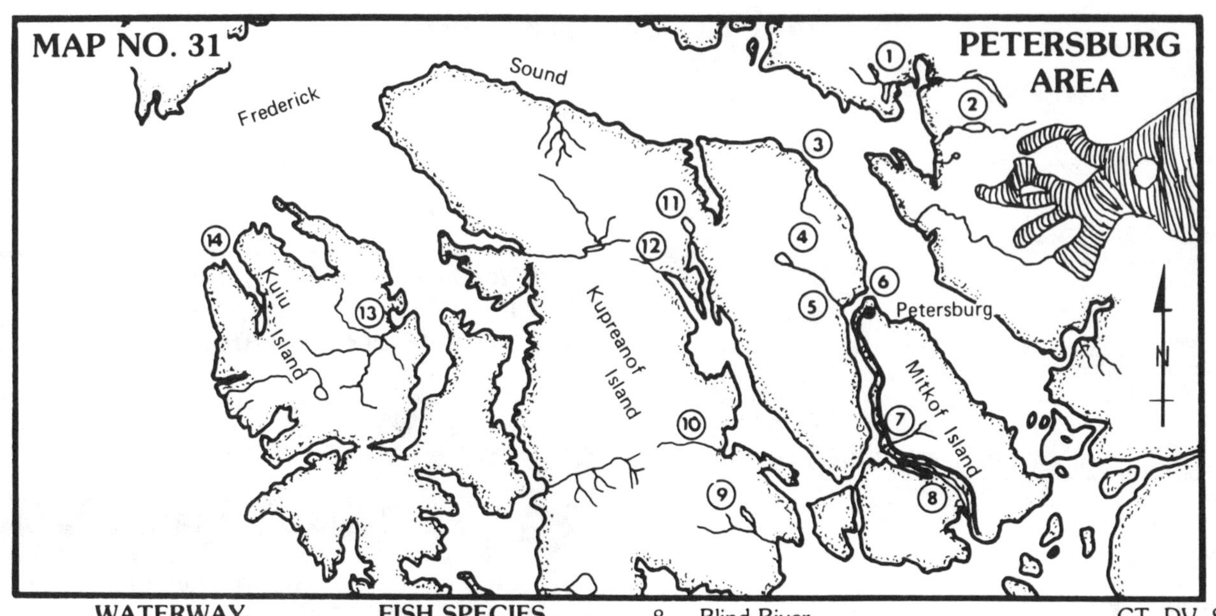

KEY NO.	WATERWAY	FISH SPECIES
1	DeBoer Lake	RT
2	Swan Lake	RT
3	Cape Strait	KS, SS, H, RF, LC
4	Petersburg Lake	DV, CT, SS
5	Petersburg Creek	CT, DV, SS, SH, CS, RT, RS, PS
6	Frederick Sound	KS, SS
7	Falls Creek	SS, PS, CS, CT, DV, SH
8	Blind River	CT, DV, SS, KS, SH
9	Kah Sheets Creek	SH, CT, DV, SS, PS, CS, RS
10	Castle River	RT, SH, CT, DV, SS, PS, CS
11	Salt Chuck	CT, DV, SS, SH
12	Towers Lake	CT, DV
13	Kadake Creek	SH, CT, DV, SS, CS, PS
14	Security Bay	KS, SS, H, RF, LC

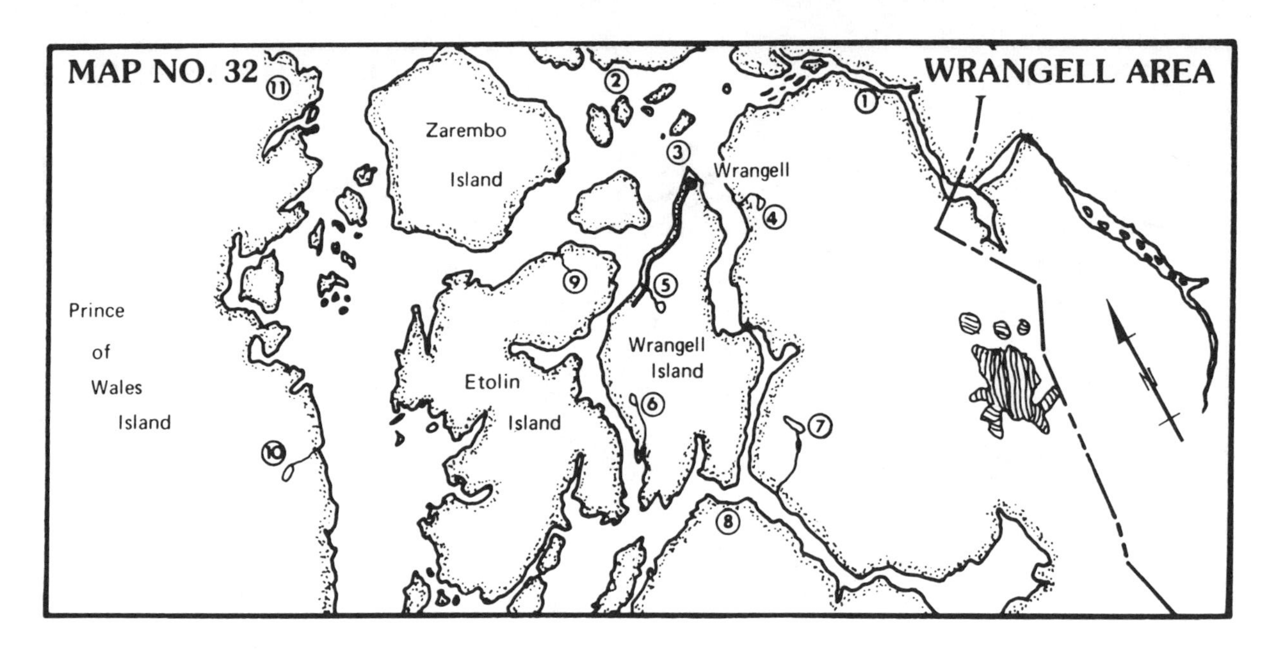

KEY NO.	WATERWAY	FISH SPECIES
1	Stikine River	SH, CT, DV, SS, PS, CS, WF, Sturgeon
2	Greys Pass	KS, H
3	Wrangell Harbor	KS, SS, H, RF
4	Virginia Lake	CT, DV, RS
5	Pats Creek & Lake	CT, DV, SS
6	Thoms Lake	CT, SS, RS, SH
7	Marten Lake	DV, RT, CT
8	Anan Creek	RT, SH, CT, DV, PS, CS, RS, SS
9	Kunk Lake	CT, DV, SS, SH
10	Luck Lake	RT, SH, CT, DV, SS, PS, RS, CS
11	Salmon Bay Lake	RT, SH, CT, DV, RS, CS, PS, SS

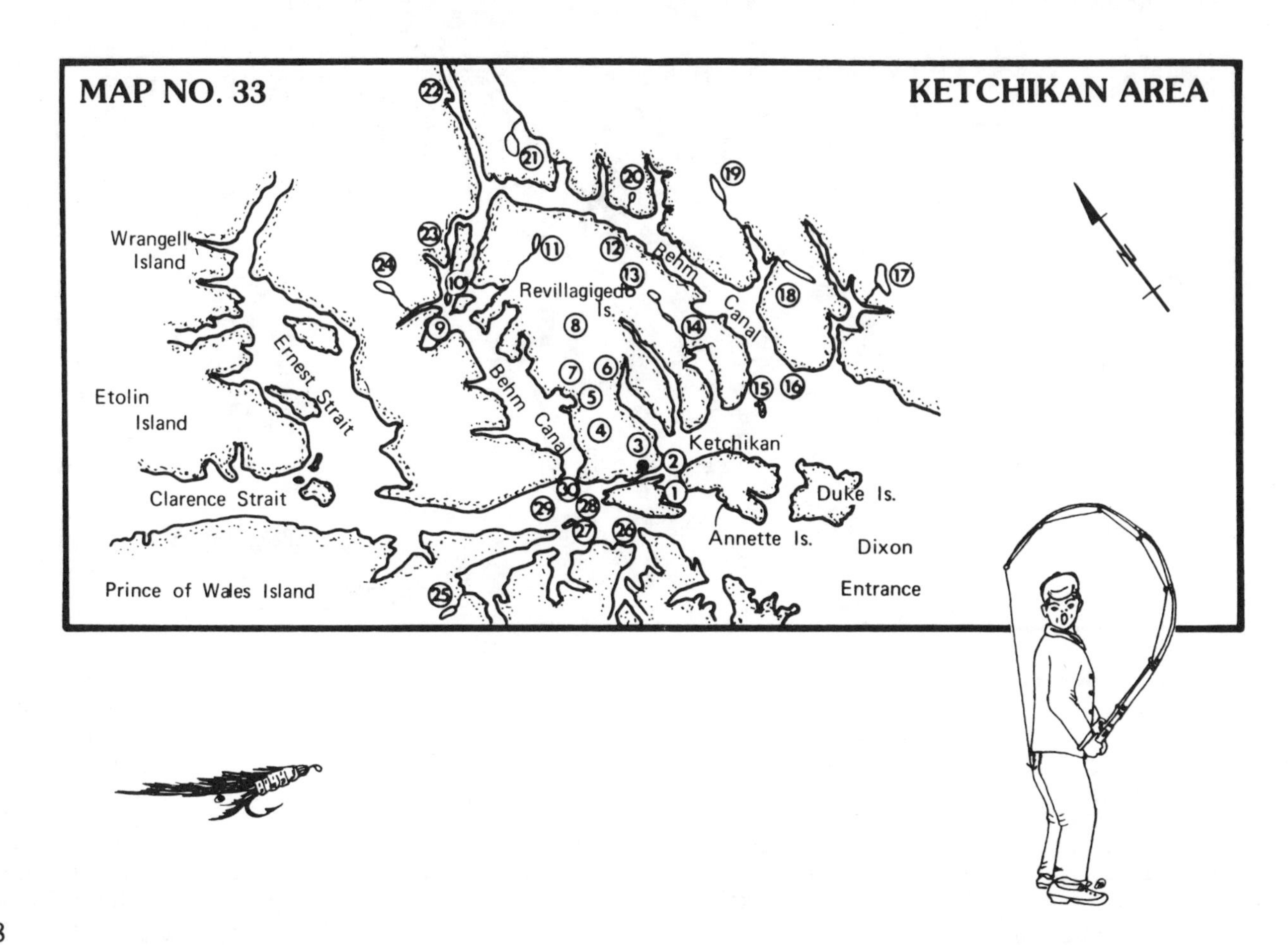
MAP NO. 33
KETCHIKAN AREA
Wrangell Island
Etolin Island
Clarence Strait
Prince of Wales Island
Ernest Strait
Behm Canal
Revillagigedo Is.
Ketchikan
Duke Is.
Annette Is.
Dixon Entrance
1
2
3
4
5
6
7
8
9
10
11
12
13
14
15
16
17
18
19
20
21
22
23
24
25
26
27
28
29
30

MAP NO. 33 KETCHIKAN AREA (Continued)

KEY NO.	WATERWAY	FISH SPECIES
1	Blank Inlet	KS, SS, PS, CS, RF, LC, H
2	Mountain Point	KS, SS, PS, CS, RF, LC, H
3	Ward Cove Creek & Lakes	RT, SH, DV, BT, CS, SS, CT, RS
4	Silvis Lake	RT
5	Harriet Hunt Lake	RT
6	Salt Lagoon Creek	RT, SH, DV, CT, SS, PS, CS
7	Naha River	GR, RT, SH, CT, DV, SS, PS, RS, CS
8	Patching Lake	GR, CT, DV
9	Yes Bay	KS, PS, CS, SS, SH, CT, DV, H, RF
10	Bell Island	KS, PS, CS, SS, SH, CT, DV, H, RF
11	Orchard Lake	CT, DV
12	Grace Lake	BT
13	Manzanita Lake	CT, DV
14	Fish Creek	RT, SH, CT, DV, SS, PS, RS
15	Point Alava	KS, SS, PS, CS, RF, LC, H
16	Point Sykes	KS, SS, PS, CS, RF, LC, H
17	Humpback Lake	GR, CT, DV
18	Bakewell Lake	CT, DV
19	Wilson Lake	CT, DV
20	Big Goat Lake	GT
21	Leduc Lake	RT
22	Unuk River	RT, SS, PS, CS, SH, CT, DV
23	Reflection Lake	RT, SH, CT, SS
24	McDonald Lake	RT, SH, CT, DV, SS, GR, RS
25	Karta River	RT, SH, CT, DV, SS, PS, RS, CS
26	Chasina Point	KS, SS, PS, CS, RF, LC, H
27	Grindall Island	KS, SS, PS, CS, RF, LC, H
28	Vallenar Point	KS, SS, PS, CS, RF, LC, H
29	Caamano Point	KS, SS, PS, CS, RF, LC, H
30	Clover Pass	KS, SS, PS, CS, RF, LC, H

NOTES

NOTES

NOTES

NOTES

THE BIG ONES THAT DIDN'T GET AWAY

GOOD FISHING HOLES